CULTURE SMART!

# POLAND

## THE ESSENTIAL GUIDE TO
## CUSTOMS & CULTURE

GREGORY ALLEN AND
MAGDALENA LIPSKA

T0054374

KUPERARD

"The real voyage of discovery consists not in seeking new landscapes, but in having new eyes."

Adapted from Marcel Proust, *Remembrance of Things Past.*

ISBN 978 1 78702 330 7

British Library Cataloguing in Publication Data
A CIP catalogue entry for this book is available
from the British Library

First published in Great Britain
by Kuperard, an imprint of Bravo Ltd
59 Hutton Grove, London N12 8DS
Tel: +44 (0) 20 8446 2440
www.culturesmart.co.uk
Inquiries: publicity@kuperard.co.uk

Design Bobby Birchall
Printed in Türkiye by Elma Basim

The Culture Smart! series is continuing to expand.
All Culture Smart! guides are available as e-books, and many
as audio books. For further information and latest titles visit
www.culturesmart.co.uk

## ABOUT THE AUTHORS

**GREGORY ALLEN, Ph.D.**, is a sociologist and Senior Lecturer in Organizational Behavior at Anglia Ruskin University in Cambridge, England, specializing in cross-cultural management, workplace diversity, and critical management studies. His doctoral thesis explored the perceptions of expatriate managers based in Poland—a topic on which he has written for both academic and industry-related publications. Originally from Canada, Gregory lived and worked in Poland for twelve years with his Polish wife, before settling in the UK.

**MAGDALENA LIPSKA** was born in Brwinow, Poland, and works in Warsaw as an interpreter, translator, and tutor in English and Japanese. She has an M.A. in Japanese studies from Warsaw University, complemented by a year of further studies at Osaka University on a scholarship from the Japanese government. A typical Polish millennial, raised on the Internet, Magda has traveled extensively and gained invaluable first-hand intercultural experience.

# CONTENTS

The Culture Smart! guides set out to equip travelers with vital information about the values and attitudes of the people they will meet, and practical advice on how to make the most of their visit abroad. Travelers to Poland in particular, a country still in transition from its recent Communist past, need to be open-minded and well-informed. Despite sweeping changes to its economic, cultural, and political landscape, the essential spirit of Poland endures. The undulating countryside, the passion and delicacy of Chopin, and the crisp mornings of the golden Polish fall continue to inspire Poles and visitors alike. Along with a certain romanticism inherited from their aristocracy, another product of Polish history has been their stubborn resistance and pride, which has often had dire consequences. Happily, Poland has turned a corner from its troubled past and is now coming to grips with the new realities of Europe and indeed of the modern world. Now is a fascinating time to get to know Poland as it strives to redefine itself within the European family.

Today's Poland is very much a mix of the old and the new, and the two are not always in harmony. *Culture Smart! Poland* provides a guide to its lasting traditions, its Communist legacy, and the more recent political and societal divisions. Background knowledge of the land, people, and history is crucial to an understanding of the Polish character: the Polish sense of identity has been forged by history, and the reader is introduced to the main events of Poland's turbulent past. The chapter on values and attitudes provides insights into this relationship-based society, and will prepare you for the specific nature of Polish social and business life. Other chapters show you where and how to meet local people and establish good relations, how Poles behave in everyday life, and how they celebrate special occasions. There are tips on coping with linguistic hurdles and how to negotiate the transportation infrastructure. The business chapter provides key information aimed at making your time in Poland as successful as it will be enjoyable.

More than anything else, Polish people are warm and generous, and place great value on personal relationships. Do not pass up an opportunity to visit them in their homes. Their hospitality is legendary. The Poles say, "A guest in the home is God in the home." *Culture Smart! Poland* will help you to become a better visitor and a welcome guest in their country.

Finally, a brief word on spelling and pronunciation. Polish has a number of unique characters and letter combinations. "Ł," as in Łódź, sounds like an English "w." The letter "w" is pronounced like an English "v," and "s" or "sz" are pronounced "sh," as in Warszawa. "Ć" or "cz," as in Częstochowa, are pronounced "ch." And "rz," as in Rzeszów, sounds like the "s" in casual.

| Official Name | The Republic of Poland (Rzeczpospolita Polska) | |
|---|---|---|
| Capital City | Warsaw (Warszawa) | Population 1.723 million |
| Other Major Cities | Kraków, Łodz, Wrocław, Poznań, Gdańsk | |
| Borders | Belarus, Czech Republic, Germany, Lithuania, Russia (Kaliningrad enclave), Slovakia, Ukraine | |
| Area | 120,628 sq. miles (312,700 sq. km) | Slightly smaller than Germany |
| Climate | Continental, with small moderating influence from the Baltic Sea in the north | |
| Currency | Zloty (PLN) 1 zloty = 100 groszy | |
| Population | 37,992,000 (2023) | 63% urban population |
| Ethnic Makeup | Polish 97.6%, German 1.3%, Ukrainian 0.6%, Belarusian 0.5% | |
| Language | Polish | Russian, English, and German are popular second languages. |
| Religion | Roman Catholic 95% | Eastern Orthodox, Protestant, and other 5% |

| | | |
|---|---|---|
| **Government** | Parliamentary republic. The Head of State is the President. Parliament has two chambers: the Sejm and Senat. | |
| **Media** | Television and radio are mixed private and public. The state broadcasters are Polskie Radio and Telewizja Polska. | The leading newspapers are *Gazeta Wyborcza* and *Rzeczpospolita* (both broadsheets), as well as *Fakt* and *Super Express* (both tabloids). |
| **Media: English Language** | *The Warsaw Voice*, *Warsaw Business Journal*, *Warsaw Insider* | Foreign newspapers can be bought at kiosks in large cities. |
| **Electricity** | 220 volts, 50 Hz (standard for continental Europe) | Buy adapters for US appliances before traveling. |
| **Video/TV** | PAL/SECAM (standard for continental Europe) | |
| **Internet Domain** | .pl | |
| **Telephone** | The country code for Poland is 48. The Warsaw area code is 22. | For long-distance calling from Poland, dial 0 then the country code. |
| **Time Zone** | Central European (CET). One hour ahead of Greenwich Mean Time (GMT +1). Six hours ahead of US Eastern Standard Time (EST+ 6) | |

# CHAPTER ONE

# LAND & PEOPLE

Welcome to Poland, the historical bridge between East and West at the heart of Europe. Poland is a relatively large European country, with an area of 120,628 square miles (312,700 sq. km); it is slightly smaller than Germany and slightly larger than Italy. With a population of 37.9 million it is the fifth most populous of the European Union's twenty-seven member states.

Poland is a land of contrasts. One of the newer members of the EU, with a growing, increasingly high-tech economy, it still has a massive agricultural sector in which farming methods have changed little over the centuries. The long Baltic coast to the north gives way to a wide central plain, and in the south are the rocky peaks of the Tatry Mountains. Even the climate is one of contrasts, with hot summers and cold, snowy winters. The large cities, such as Warsaw, Kraków, Gdańsk, and Wrocław, with their bright lights, modern facilities, and nightlife, are in stark contrast to the backward villages of the countryside, where time appears to have stood still for a hundred years. While most younger Poles have embraced a modern, Western lifestyle, many of the older generation remain very traditional. This contrast exists not only on a macro scale but also within individuals—even educated, forward-looking young people are rooted in a strong sense of tradition.

Walking through the centers of Warsaw, Kraków, Gdańsk, or Poznań today, it is hard to believe that not so long ago this was a bankrupt Communist state. Polish city centers are full of shops, boutiques, cafés, restaurants, pubs, and clubs. The cafés of Kraków and Wrocław are every bit as charming and distinctive as those of Paris or Madrid. This is in stark contrast to the rural countryside. While many of Poland's large cities have enjoyed the fruits of EU membership and a growing economy, the countryside has not. In many small villages little has changed in the past twenty years, except for a slide into neglect and the migration of the youth abroad or to more prosperous Polish towns and cities.

Never feel shy about asking Poles to describe the changes that have transformed their country and society. In fact, there is often no need to ask, as many Poles are just as keen to share their views as they are to hear a foreigner's.

## GEOGRAPHICAL OVERVIEW

Poland is bordered to the west by Germany, to the south by the Czech and Slovak Republics, to the east by

Mountain hut in the scenic Gąsienicowa Valley in the Tatry Mountains.

Ukraine, Belarus, and Lithuania, and to the northeast by the tiny Russian enclave of Kaliningrad. The Baltic Sea defines the northern border.

The country is dominated by a large, central plain that encompasses the cities of Warsaw, Poznań, and Łódź. The port city of Gdańsk is located on the Baltic. The entire southern region is mountainous, with the highest peaks of the Tatry Mountains, 70 miles (113 km) south of Kraków, reaching an elevation of 8,200 feet (2,499 m). Two major rivers, the Vistula (Wisła ) and the Oder (Odra), flow from the mountains in the south to the Baltic. Warsaw, Kraków, and Gdańsk were built along the Vistula. The Oder originates in the Czech Republic and flows northwest through Wrocław before forming a large part of the German–Polish border and finally meeting the Baltic near the port of Szczecin in the northwest.

The major population centers are spread throughout the country, with Warsaw lying near the middle of the central plain, geographically isolated from any notable topographic features. Due west of Warsaw, approximately 200 miles (322 km) on the highway to Berlin, is Poznań. Gdańsk on the Baltic coast lies alongside Gdynia and Sopot; collectively they are known as the Tri-City. Kraków is situated some 200 miles south of Warsaw, just north of the Tatry Mountains. Wrocław is located in the southwest of the country, north of the Sudety Mountains, which continue into the Czech Republic and eastern Germany.

## Climate

Poland has a primarily continental climate, tempered by the Baltic Sea in the north. Summers are typically hot and sunny, and the time when city residents flee in droves to the countryside, lakes, seaside, or mountains. The hot weather normally lasts from late May till early September, although this varies greatly from year to year.

| AVERAGE DAILY TEMPERATURES FOR SELECTED MONTHS | | |
|---|---|---|
| Warsaw | Fahrenheit | Celsius |
| January | 27° | -2° |
| April | 46° | 7° |
| July | 67° | 19° |
| October | 48° | 9° |

Fall can range from dark and gloomy to stunningly beautiful. The famous Polish golden fall has a deserved reputation. Perhaps the best words to describe Warsaw winters are gray and damp. These are in stark contrast to the snowy peaks of the mountainous south where the food, hospitality, and mulled beer should not be missed!

## A BRIEF HISTORY

> "To be defeated and not submit, that is victory; to be victorious and rest on one's laurels, that is defeat."
>
> Marshal Józef Piłsudski (1867–1935),
> Polish commander-in-chief
> and statesman

Few countries have been more fought over than Poland. The Russians, Prussians, Tatars, Turks, Swedes, Austrians, and Germans have all fought over this land. That the Polish nation exists at all today is a testament to the resilience and character of the people.

History shapes the mindset of any nation, but this point has a special significance in the case of Poland. The suppression of their culture, traditions, religion, and language in various periods of their history has had a strong effect on the way Poles view themselves and their relations with others. From their checkered past has come the Poles' indomitable spirit. They have lost many battles but not the war, and their vibrant culture and economy are proof of this.

Today's Poles are very conscious of their history and take great pride in their heritage and culture, which has been interwoven with the Catholic faith. Their national identity has largely been forged by the Church, which continues to be very influential in modern Polish society.

The Polish perception of their own history is far from objective, however. They focus on and take inspiration from the resilience of their ancestors and the continuity of their culture through the centuries. This has all too often had the effect of turning Poland into an introverted nation, detached, politically and psychologically, from the rest of Europe. Following the signing of the European Union Accession Treaty in May 2004, EU membership and steady economic growth had a positive impact on Poland's reengagement with the rest of the continent. Recent years, however, have seen a significant growth in populist anti-EU sentiment, often linked with right-wing political parties.

Through the prism of their historical narrative, the Poles see themselves as a strong, noble people who have consistently been on the morally correct side of conflicts, if not always on the victorious side. This has contributed to a self-image of victimhood. Rather than expecting support from beyond their borders, the Poles learned to cope alone as best they could. Even today, foreigners in Poland are often told how the rest of the world has repeatedly abandoned Poland in its hour of need.

The following section outlines some of the most important developments in the history of the Polish people.

## Origins

Little is known about the origins of Poland's earliest
inhabitants. It is thought that they were a mixture of
hunter-gatherers and farmers, who helped develop the
first trade routes through the region. The remains of
a fortified settlement from the eighth century BCE at
Biskupin, in north-central Poland, were unearthed in
the 1930s and can be visited today. These ancient trade
routes included the lucrative "Amber Road," linking
the Baltic Sea to Rome and the Mediterranean, which
dates back to the fifth century BCE.

Around the fifth century BCE Celtic and Germanic
tribes, among others, started launching raids into the
area. In response to these attacks, the native settlers
and nomads began to organize themselves into larger
groups. In time these groups came to include the
Slavs, believed to have arrived in Polish territory in
the sixth or seventh century CE, having migrated
westward from the region of modern-day Belarus
while other Slavic tribes moved south and east.

Living outside the borders of the Roman Empire,
the peoples of the area were less advanced than
their neighbors to the south and west. Nevertheless,
they lived in tribal communities with clear power
structures, administrative centers, and trading
settlements. With the increase in trade, the Slavs
of the region thrived and one of their groups, the
Polanie, eventually settled in Poland's central plain,
laying the foundations of what would become the
Polish nation.

### The Piast Dynasty

From the ninth century, the Polanie were ruled by the Piast Dynasty, which ushered in the beginnings of Polish nationhood. Under Piast rule, Polish language and culture began to flourish.

Christianity came in 966 CE with the baptism of the Piast prince Mieszko I, who wisely chose to accept Christianity directly from Rome and thus avoid the forced conversion of his pagan people by the Frankish German Empire. The Polish Church was established in the year 1000, under the direct control and protection of Rome. The first Polish king, Bolesław I, "the Brave," was crowned twenty-five years later, thus establishing the Kingdom of Poland.

In an incident bearing a striking similarity to the later assassination of Thomas à Becket at the behest of Henry II of England, in 1079 Stanislaw, the Bishop of Kraków, was murdered while celebrating Mass by Bolesław II, "the Bold." This followed a series of rebellions against Bolesław in which Stanisław had taken a leading role. These events set a precedent of the Church finding itself at odds with the ruling power of the time, a pattern that would recur through the centuries, often with dire consequences.

In the year 1226, Duke Konrad of Mazovia, who was under attack from pagan Baltic tribes, requested assistance from the Teutonic Knights, a German crusading military order that would have a significant and lasting influence on Poland. The Knights eventually turned on the Poles and gained control over the area of Prussia, depriving Poland of access to the sea. Their impressive architectural skills can be seen in their massive castle in Marienburg, present-day Malbork (a destination not to be missed!). In addition, the port of Gdańsk (Danzig), which had previously been controlled by a local Slav dynasty, was conquered and subsequently developed in this period. In taking Gdańsk, the Teutonic Knights slaughtered the local population and invited German settlers into the city.

## The Tatar Invasions

Another great but devastating foreign influence came from the Tatars, who first invaded Poland in 1241. The Tatars were nomadic Mongolian warriors from Central Asia, feared for their horsemanship and archery skills. Although they owed allegiance to the Mongol Empire founded by Genghis Khan, the Tatars operated independently, launching raids into Russian, Polish, Czech, and Hungarian territory and returning with their spoils to the steppe lands of Central Asia.

The invasions were swift and destructive. Villages were plundered and burned, and those who could fled far from their homes. Polish defenses proved no match for these skilled horsemen, and the great Polish cities of Legnica and Kraków were destroyed.

The rebuilding process that followed the Tatar invasions saw the development of a number of towns that were largely inhabited by foreign settlers. Germans introduced their own culture and traditions as well as their skills in a variety of trades. Another minority group that grew in size during this period was the Jews. They contributed to the economic growth of the kingdom despite the Catholic Church's displeasure at the tolerance shown them by Bolesław the Pious, who granted them a General Charter of Liberties in 1264.

## Kazimierz the Great

Toward the end of the Piast Dynasty, Kraków flourished as the capital under King Kazimierz III (1333–70). Better known as Kazimierz the Great, he was to be the last of the Piast kings. It was in this period that one of Europe's first universities was established in Kraków. It still exists today as the Jagiełłonian University, one of the country's most prestigious academic institutions.

The year 1331 saw the first sitting of the Polish parliament, the Sejm (pronounced "same"). Kazimierz III greatly extended Poland's borders and oversaw the writing of the country's first legal code. The country, and Kraków in particular, thrived thanks largely to the bustling east–west and north–south trade routes that crossed through Poland. It is said that Kazimierz "found Poland built of wood and left her built of stone."

## The Jagiełłonian Dynasty (1386–1572)

Without a male heir, Kazimierz the Great left the throne to his nephew, Louis the Great of Hungary. After much confusion as to who should sit on the Polish throne, Louis' crown eventually passed to his eleven-year-old daughter, Jadwiga, in 1384. Jadwiga wed the Grand Duke of Lithuania, Jagiełło, in 1386, who accepted Christianity on behalf of his nation and was baptized as Wladyslaw II Jagiełło. This personal dynastic union acted to protect Lithuania from the Teutonic Knights, whose mission it was to forcibly convert the pagan peoples of Eastern

Europe. The marriage marked the beginning of the Polish–Lithuanian union, perhaps the only successful such union in Polish history, and created what was the largest country in Europe. It helped to keep both the Tatars and the Teutonic Knights at bay, while extending the kingdom's borders from the Baltic to the Black Sea.

### The Battle of Grunwald (Tannenberg)

Mongol invasions plagued Poland through the thirteenth century, but in the fifteenth century a group of Tatars came to Poland's aid. In the summer of 1410, Jagiełło led a mixed army of Poles, Lithuanians, Orthodox Christians, Tatars, and Bohemian Hussites to a long-awaited victory over the Teutonic Knights in the battle of Grunwald.

The German Order had enlisted the help of various Western European countries to combat the "pagan" Lithuanians and their Polish supporters. In fact, many of the Lithuanians who took part in the battle of Grunwald had not yet embraced Christianity, not to mention the Muslim Tatar troops. Although they comprised a minority of the forces, for Poles Grunwald is a symbol of victory in the face of oppression. Local villagers armed with nothing more than wooden clubs helped swell the numbers and joined in to defeat the military might of the Teutonic Knights with their superior weaponry and skills. Poland was finally free of this menace and the subsequent peace saw the Polish–Lithuanian Union increase its share of the region, although the Teutonic Knights were permitted to retain their stronghold at Marienburg.

The battle of Grunwald. An illustration from the fifteenth-century Chronicle of Berne.

With Jagiełłonians briefly holding power concurrently in Hungary and Bohemia as well as Poland–Lithuania, their combined empire not only stretched from the Baltic to the Black Sea but came within a stone's throw of Moscow. This massive territory contained a variety of ethnic groups including Poles, Lithuanians, Estonians, Ukrainians, Prussians, Muslim Tatars, and Jews.

## Religious Tolerance

Poland was known as a land of religious tolerance where each group could practice its faith without fear of persecution. Between the twelfth and fifteenth centuries Jews came in large numbers from the west—mostly from German lands and Bohemia—escaping the persecution and massacres that accompanied the Crusades and the Black Death, and later following their expulsion from Spain. Unlike the largely peasant Slavic population, they were city dwellers and craftsmen, experienced in trade and fiscal matters. For these reasons Polish kings and princes encouraged them to settle and offered them protection. Occasioned by Poland's need for merchants and tradesmen, this influx resulted in a thriving Jewish community. Another ethnic minority, the Prussians, were granted considerable autonomy in order to provide the skills needed to drive economic expansion.

### The Renaissance in Poland

While the cultural explosion of the Renaissance for the most part passed neighboring Russia by, Polish arts and sciences flourished during this period, with many influential thinkers taking advantage of Poland's tolerance of ideas not supported by the Church. The sixteenth century was a "Golden Age" of cultural, academic, and economic

Monument to Copernicus in front of the Polish Academy of Sciences in Warsaw.

activity. Nicholas Copernicus (Mikołaj Kopernik) published *On the Revolutions of the Celestial Spheres*, postulating that the Earth revolved around the Sun. Polish art, architecture, and literature were strongly influenced by Renaissance Italy.

## The Royal Republic

In 1569 the Polish parliament, or Sejm, enacted the Union of Lublin, formally uniting Poland and Lithuania into the Polish Commonwealth. The period of Jagiełłonian rule in Poland ended with Zygmunt August, who died in 1572 without an heir. This was followed by the so-called Republic of Nobles, which introduced elective succession, with the nobility electing the new king. Corruption reigned supreme in the process, with votes being openly bought and sold, resulting ultimately in a series of foreign rulers and sowing the seeds of the destruction of Poland as a strong European power. In a period when other European countries were moving toward more centralized government, Poland was ruled by a feudal nobility and becoming increasingly regionally divided. The Poles were proving a difficult lot to govern and there was little allegiance to the elected monarchs, foreign or Polish.

There were, however, victories for the Polish army in this period, most notably the defeat of Ivan the Terrible of Russia. Stefan Batory of Transylvania, husband of Anna Jagiełłon, who had temporarily held the throne until she married, led Poland to battle over the contested land of Livonia (roughly modern-day Latvia) in 1571. Were it not for interference from

Rome, Batory may well have taken Moscow, so complete was his victory over the Russians.

The third of the elected rulers, the Swedish Zygmunt III, moved the capital from Kraków to Warsaw in 1596, an act for which Krakovians have not forgiven him to this day.

## The Reformation and Counter-Reformation

It is a common misconception that the Roman Catholic Church remained unchallenged in its spiritual domination of Poland throughout its thousand-year history in the country. By the middle of the sixteenth century, the Sejm was dominated by Protestant princes who had curtailed the power of the Church. As we have seen, Poland had adopted an official position of religious tolerance. This resulted, among other things, in Lutheran Livonia seeking Polish protection from Orthodox Russia. The region in return became Polish territory. With many of the Polish nobility having converted to Protestantism, and with the Germanic regions of the country being strongly Lutheran, Poland looked to be following the lead of her Western neighbors on the road to becoming a Protestant nation. One key factor was missing, however. There was no effective native professional or middle class of tradesmen and skilled workers. Poland remained stubbornly entrenched in the feudal system.

This marks the beginning of a trend that would have a profound effect on Polish society throughout the following centuries. While a skilled and literate middle class was growing in countries to the West, no sizable equivalent existed in Poland (hence the need to import skilled Jewish and German merchants and tradesmen). It was the urban middle class that was fueling the Reformation in the West, and this was lacking in Poland. The popularity of the reformist movement in Poland was almost exclusively an upper-class phenomenon, while the peasants remained loyal to the Catholic Church.

The Counter-Reformation was a largely bloodless victory for the Catholics. The Polish Church was reformed and Jesuits opened schools and helped to regain what trust the Church had previously lost. The defining moment came in 1564 when King Zygmunt (Sigmund) II, who had previously favored Protestantism, was persuaded to accept the Catholic faith. Protestants were subsequently neither expelled nor persecuted. The official position of religious tolerance remained in place, although the Jesuits were encouraged to convert the remaining pockets of Protestantism. The Orthodox Cossacks of Ukraine were also targeted for conversion, which was partly responsible for the Cossack uprising of 1648.

The position of the Catholic Church in Poland was strengthened in the second half of the seventeenth century when the Protestant Charles X of Sweden invaded, sacking churches and monasteries, and committing atrocities against the general population. These attacks were largely seen by the Poles as being Protestant versus Catholic in nature, rather than as an opportunistic land grab.

### *Potop* (The Deluge)

In 1648, the so-called *potop*, or deluge, began with Poland being attacked simultaneously by Swedes, Tatars, and Cossacks. Poland's vulnerability was largely the result of petty infighting among the quarrelsome and proud nobility. This period has been immortalized, if in a rather nationalistic way, in the epic novel *Potop* by Henryk Sienkiewicz (1846–1916). After the Swedes had ransacked most of the country, the Poles regrouped and mounted an impressive offensive, regaining much of the lost territory. Poles would recall the *potop* frequently in their later history as an example of how they could turn the tables on foreign invasion and oppression. Peace with Sweden was secured by the Treaty of Oliwa in 1660, but Poland–Lithuania lay in ruins with enemies across each border. The landmass of the Commonwealth was greatly reduced and nearly half the population had died through war and disease.

Arguably, Poland's finest hour militarily came in 1683 when King Jan III Sobieski convincingly defeated the Ottoman Turks as they made their way through the Balkans and on to Vienna. Many Poles still regard this as the moment they "saved" Christian Europe from Muslim rule. The Austrians, however, had an eye on Galicia in southern Poland, and before long the two states would find themselves at war.

Back at home the Commonwealth continued crumbling, due largely to nepotism, the dysfunctional political structure, and bitter infighting between groups of nobles. As central political power was further eroded, Poland's neighbors began to set their sights on her. Russia in particular, under the reigns of Peter the Great (1682–1725) and Catherine the Great (1762–96), increasingly exploited her divisions to gain influence in Warsaw.

## The Partitions

For the period 1795–1916, Poland was absent from the map of Europe. In a series of three partitions, the enfeebled state was divided between Peter the Great's Russia, Frederick II's Kingdom of Prussia, and Maria Theresa's Austrian Empire. Each of these powerful empires had territorial ambitions and their weak and divided neighbor provided a tempting opportunity.

The first partition, in 1772, was a tactical move proposed by Frederick II to secure lands that Peter the Great had set his sights on, thereby avoiding a Russian–Austrian war. The three powers agreed to divide Poland in such a way that a balance would be achieved between them and war averted. Under the first partition, the northern and central regions of Pomerelia (later Eastern Pomerania) and Ermeland were ceded to Prussia; Belarus and Latgale (in eastern Latvia) in the east to Russia; and the southern region of Galicia to Austria.

After losing about a third of Poland's territory and half its inhabitants in the first partition, King Stanisław August together with the Sejm took steps toward political reform in an attempt to avoid further loss of control. These reforms culminated in Europe's first written constitution, the second in the world after the USA. The May 3 Constitution is a source of pride for Poles and is marked by a national holiday.

Provoked by the Polish constitution, Russia moved against the new government and instigated the second partition of Poland in 1793. This partition enlarged the Russian sector to the east and the Prussian sector to the west, including Gdańsk, while leaving Poland with a small fragment of its former lands.

### The Kościuszko Uprising

In 1794 in an attempt to reclaim Polish honor after capitulation in the first two partitions, Tadeusz Kościuszko led an army composed mainly of peasants armed with scythes against the Russians. Kościuszko, a military engineer and hero of the American War of Independence, and his peasant troops mounted an impressive offensive, but it was never going to be enough to defeat the

Tadeusz Kościuszko, military engineer, statesman, and national hero.

Russians. The insurrection gave Catherine the Great the opportunity to finish the process begun with the first partition and end the existence of the Polish state in 1795.

### Napoleon Bonaparte

A brief respite from complete foreign domination came in the form of Napoleon Bonaparte. Recognizing that a victory for Napoleon over their occupiers offered them the best chance to regain their independence, the Poles rallied behind the French emperor both at home and abroad. For their support, however, the only independence they were granted was the semi-autonomous Duchy of Warsaw, created in 1807 out of Polish lands that Napoleon had captured from the Prussians. When the French troops retreated before the advancing Russians, the Duchy of Warsaw was quickly recaptured and put under Russian control.

The postwar Congress of Vienna in 1815 offered little to Poles hoping for autonomy in part of what had been their vast country. The occupying powers reestablished their control. The Duchy of Warsaw was ceded to Russia as a semi-independent state called the Congress Kingdom of Poland, with the Russian Tsar as King of Poland. Kraków was made a "free city" within Austrian-held Galicia. Guarantees of home rule in all parts of the divided country, and of free communication between them, were given by all three occupying powers, only to prove empty.

### Nationalism and Rebellion

The Poles constantly struggled for national liberation. The so-called November Uprising of 1830 against the Russian occupiers was centered in what had been the Duchy of Warsaw. The new Russian Tsar, Nicholas I, responded with a heavy hand, crushing the insurgents and enacting new laws effectively outlawing Polish language and culture in

an attempt to Russianize the population. The inability
of the Polish intelligentsia to gain the support of the
peasants in the countryside prevented the uprising
from growing into a full-scale insurrection. Many of
those who could emigrated in this period to escape
a dire economic situation and intensified Russian
oppression. The years 1846 and 1863 saw other failed
insurrections, after which many insurgents were exiled
to Siberia.

The Polish adage about the best coming out
through suffering was proved true in this period.
A cultural revival took place under this repressive
occupation. Most notable examples were the
composer Frédéric (Fryderyk) Chopin (1810–49) and
the Romantic poets Adam Mickiewicz (1798–1855)

Portrait (detail) of Adam Mickiewicz, 1828.

Chopin. Watercolor and ink portrait, 1836.

and Juliusz Słowacki (1809–49). These artists drew on the plight of their nation as a source of inspiration and are still held in extremely high regard.

### The Industrial Revolution in Poland

The rise of capitalism and industrialization in the latter half of the nineteenth century had profound effects on Polish society. One of these was a mass migration to the cities, as peasants left the land and sought work in the growing number of factories and coal mines. The cities of Katowice and Łódź developed in this period. The mobility and growing economic power of the peasants undermined the hold of the Polish nobility.

Millions of Poles emigrated in this period, mainly to the USA, in search of a better life without the economic hardship and political oppression of their homeland. In 1892 the Polish Socialist Party was founded by Józef Piłsudski, who is often referred to as the "father of the Second Polish Republic."

### The First World War

The First World War was devastating for each of the three powers occupying Poland. As much of the fighting took place on Polish soil, it was devastating for Poland as well, with an estimated one million Poles dead by the war's end. The war did, however, provide the opportunity for Poland to become a sovereign state once again. At the insistence of US President Woodrow Wilson, the postwar settlement was based upon the principle of national self-determination. In

November 1918 an independent Polish republic was established, with Józef Piłsudski as president.

Following the Treaty of Versailles in 1919, the newly drawn borders of Poland resulted in East Prussia being cut off from Germany by the so-called "Polish corridor," which gave Poland access to the Baltic. The port of Gdańsk, or Danzig as the Germans referred to it, was given the status of a free, trading city-state. The population of Gdańsk remained predominantly German. The Polish Constitution of 1921 protected the rights of national minorities.

## The Polish–Soviet War

With Lenin looking to spread Marxism westward and Marshal Piłsudski aiming to regain historic Polish

Marshal Piłsudski in a portrait by Edward Okuń, 1919.

territory in the east, war was inevitable. In 1919–21
Polish forces advanced into newly independent
Lithuania, seizing control of its capital Vilnius, and into
Ukraine as far as Kiev. Then Poland's own independence
came under threat as the Red Army approached to
within a few miles of Warsaw. Piłsudski's August 1920
counteroffensive, known as "the miracle on the Vistula,"
however, drove it back more than three hundred miles
into Ukraine. The subsequent peace, signed in Riga in
1921, saw Poland and Russia divide much of Ukraine
and Belarus between themselves. On its other front,
Poland managed to keep Vilnius.

### The Interwar Period

The period between the First and Second World Wars
is regarded by many Poles as the country's cultural
coming of age, and an age that was stolen from them
by the events that were to follow. Warsaw residents,
in particular, are fond of telling stories of their city's
international appeal during this all-too-brief period
of peace and prosperity.

The first parliamentary governments of the Polish
Republic consisted of right-wing and centrist parties.
They faced a country in ruins after six years of war
and tried, unsuccessfully, to create a stable currency,
jobs for millions of unemployed, and a *modus vivendi*
with national minorities and neighboring states.
There was widespread discontent and civil disorder.
In 1926, Piłsudski, frustrated by the incompetence
of parliament, seized full power in a military coup,
effectively making Poland a military dictatorship.

He had the support of his people, however, and under his direction the economy was revived and the country, divided for so long, began to rebuild itself. On his death in 1935, a military regime held power under Marshal Śmigły-Rydz.

Rising feelings of nationalism further strained relations between Poles and their minority communities. Poland had Europe's largest Jewish population, numbering 3.5 million souls. Unease over the Nazi persecution of German Jews was tangible, and worried not only Poland's Jews but also many Poles who feared the German *Führer* would not tolerate a massive Jewish presence in his backyard and would use this as a pretext for aggression. In the late 1930s a wave of anti-Jewish pogroms swept Poland, and boycotts were organized against Jewish businesses. Many Polish liberals honorably provided moral and political support for the Jews in this difficult time.

Dark clouds were gathering on the horizon. Poland was flanked by two countries ruled by aggressive dictators: Stalin to the east and Hitler to the south and west, following the annexation of Czechoslovakia in May 1938. Ominously, Stalin and Hitler had secretly signed a nonaggression pact according to which, theoretically at least, each party was free to invade Poland from its respective side without fear of interference from the other. With Poland thus surrounded and Hitler's concept of *Lebensraum* already being put into practice, there was only one outcome.

## The Second World War

On September 1, 1939, Hitler used the Polish refusal to renegotiate the status of Danzig and East Prussia as an excuse to launch war against his eastern neighbor. Two weeks later the Soviets invaded Poland from the east, and by the month's end the country was once again under complete foreign domination. In support of Poland, England and France declared war on Germany, but offered no immediate military aid.

While the Nazi German enslavement and slaughter of prisoners of war is well documented, many are unaware that an estimated 1,660,000 Polish soldiers and civilians were deported to labor camps by the Soviets in 1940 and 1941. Additionally, thousands of prisoners of war were executed by the Red Army as part of their agreement with Hitler to wipe the Polish state off the map of Europe. Most notorious among such incidents was the execution of at least 20,000 officers of the defeated Polish army in the forests of Katyn in March 1940. The refusal of the Soviet authorities to accept responsibility or even acknowledge the massacre was a cause of great animosity among ordinary Poles.

Germany gained complete control of Polish territory after invading the Soviet Union in June 1941. A system of concentration camps, such as Auschwitz and Treblinka, was set up by the Germans—well outside their own borders—to rid themselves of "racial inferiors" in their newly conquered lands. These death factories served both to supply slave labor for the war effort and to exterminate millions in gas chambers and by other means.

## *THE WARSAW GHETTO*

In 1939 the Nazis established a ghetto in the center of Warsaw into which 433,000 Jews were crowded. In 1942 transports to the extermination camp at Treblinka began. In April 1943 the SS were sent in to round up the remaining Jews and destroy the buildings. Rather than submit, the Jews fought back with small arms they had managed to smuggle in. Resistance continued until May. Many Jewish fighters escaped via the sewers and joined the Polish underground.

## The Warsaw Uprising

When Germany attacked the Soviet Union in 1941, the Poles and Soviets suddenly shared a common enemy. Far from becoming close allies, however, Soviet troops sat just across the Vistula from central Warsaw and watched as the Germans brought down the Warsaw Uprising of 1944.

Coordinated by the pro-Western Polish Home Army, known as the Armia Krajowa, with a mandate from the Polish Government-in-Exile in London, the uprising had begun on August 1, when the Soviet Army was advancing toward the capital. It ended as a massacre. The Western Allies put little pressure on the Soviets to help the Poles, and Stalin vetoed the Allied use of his airfields for supply drops. After sixty-three days of bitter fighting some 200,000 Poles

The ruins of Warsaw's Old Town market place in 1945.

were killed. In retaliation the Germans razed the city, leaving nothing but piles of rubble, before fleeing. The Red Army eventually liberated Poland from the Nazis in 1945. By the end of the war, 6 million Polish citizens had died, half of them Jews. In 2004, on the sixtieth anniversary of the Warsaw Uprising, the Warsaw Rising Museum was opened in the Wola district of Warsaw.

## The Postwar Settlement
At the Yalta Conference in February 1945, Stalin gained assurances from Roosevelt and Churchill that Poland would be left in the Soviet sphere of influence. After all their suffering in the war, the Poles felt betrayed by their Western allies.

Following Yalta and the Potsdam Conferences in July/August 1945, it was decided that Poland would be returned to its approximate medieval boundaries, meaning a general shift to the west of some 120 miles (193 km). Western territory was taken from Germany and eastern lands were given to the Soviet Union. This operation involved the forced mass migration of approximately 3 million Poles and 2 million Germans. The results can still be seen today in cities such as Wrocław (formerly Breslau), where the German population was completely replaced by Poles, mostly from the region of modern-day Ukraine.

## Communism

Poland was always far from being the ideal Communist state. Stalin is said to have referred to Polish Communists as resembling radishes: red on the outside but scratch a little and inside they're pure white.

It was no surprise when, in 1946, the Communists were given the green light to nationalize the country's economy in the rigged "three times yes" referendum. The following year all right-wing political parties were outlawed, and a socialist coalition was formed to govern the People's Republic of Poland with no real opposition. The People's Republic marched more or less in step with Moscow, although Polish citizens didn't have to live with secret police oppression on the scale of the East German Stasi or Russia's KGB. By 1949 the (Communist) Polish United Worker's Party (PZPR) had become the only political force in the country.

In 1949 Poland joined Comecon, the Soviet-dominated economic bloc. The early 1950s saw the introduction of harsh Stalinist rule, including further nationalization, rural collectivization, and persecution of members of the Church. In 1955 Poland joined the Warsaw Pact Soviet defense organization.

The imposition of Stalinism, however, had the effect of driving Poles toward the Catholic Church, which was effectively the only organization outside Communist control allowed by the government. There were strikes and riots in Poznań in 1956, and in the 1960s a small measure of liberalization took place. The economy languished, however, and in 1970 there were riots in Gdańsk against food price rises.

The first mass signs of discontent with the Communist system could perhaps be seen at the widespread jubilation at the election of Karol Wojtyła as Pope John Paul II in 1978. When the new pope visited his homeland a year later, he was greeted by the largest public gathering of Poles in history. The Catholic Church, which had always provided a discreet counterpoint to Communist propaganda, had suddenly come to the fore as a political force in the country.

## Solidarity and Martial Law

In 1980, a Gdańsk shipyard electrician named Lech Wałęsa led a group of workers striking against the recent 100 percent rise in the price of foodstuffs. The Solidarity Trade Union was formed and supported striking miners in Silesia as well as the workers in the port. The strikers gained widespread support, including that of the Catholic Church and opposition intellectuals. The group's demands, or twenty-one points, listed the rights that would soon be fought for throughout the Eastern bloc. By June 1980, the government had officially recognized Solidarity and made important concessions.

After giving in and granting official recognition to Solidarity, however, the Polish government came under intense pressure from Moscow and reversed this decision. In December 1981 General Jaruzelski imposed martial law. With their new sweeping powers, the military police rounded up and imprisoned Solidarity leaders and activists, including Wałęsa, and the trade union was officially disbanded. During this period civil liberties virtually ceased to exist. Tanks rumbled through the streets, roadblocks sprang up as all traffic was searched, and thousands were detained without being formally charged.

By 1982, the government hoped it had sufficiently slowed the momentum of Solidarity. Wałęsa was released and the following year martial law was lifted. Their hopes were in vain, however, as Wałęsa would receive the Nobel Peace Prize in the same year, gaining international recognition and sympathy for his struggling organization. Back home meanwhile, the murder of Father Jerzy Popiełuszko, a Solidarity sympathizer, by a secret policeman did little to rebuild trust in the beleaguered government.

At the same time as Jaruzelski was losing the struggle for popular support to Solidarity, the country was facing possibly its most severe financial crisis. Because it was on the brink of bankruptcy, all goods produced

"Thirty years of Solidarity." A mural in Ostrowiec, with Jerzy Popiełuszko in the foreground.

were exported for hard Western currency, leaving precious little for domestic consumption. Any Pole who lived through the 1980s remembers this period as a time of rationing and scarcity. Lines outside shops wound around city blocks, and many still recall rows of shelves with nothing on them but a few bottles of vinegar.

In order to maintain a decent standard of life, many people came to rely on informal networks of friends and acquaintances to acquire officially contraband goods. Such networks survive to this day and, in many cases, help to explain the way business dealings can work in this country.

## The Fall of Communism
By the late 1980s, the desperate economic state of its citizens, coupled with the wind of political change

blowing through Central and Eastern Europe, spelled the end for the Communist regime in Poland. In a last-gasp attempt to reach a compromise and avoid anarchy, General Jaruzelski invited representatives of Solidarity, including Lech Wałęsa, to participate in a series of round-table talks. The result was a compromise under which Solidarity would be legally recognized and permitted to field candidates for a limited number of seats in parliamentary elections. The writing was on the wall for the government when Solidarity candidates cruised through to easy victories in nearly all the contested seats.

For members of the Communist Party, it was a case of jumping from a sinking ship, and in 1989 the popular journalist and Solidarity advisor Tadeusz Mazowiecki was chosen to lead an interim government to oversee open presidential elections the following year. Once again in the political spotlight, Lech Wałęsa easily won the elections, becoming Poland's first post-Communist president.

The following years were difficult for most Poles as tough austerity measures took their toll, but the atmosphere was one of change and, for the most part, people were prepared to suffer today for the promise of a better tomorrow. The entrepreneurial spirit in the country began to show as seemingly everyone who could became involved in some form of business. This ranged from the setting up of local subsidiaries of prestigious Western firms to selling homegrown produce from the trunk of a car.

## European Union Membership

In May 2004 Poland became a member of the European Union, five years after joining NATO, and fifteen years after the end of Communist rule. Poland's relationship with the EU has not been an entirely harmonious one, however, with the government often at odds with the EU over infringements of EU law. This has centered mainly on issues regarding government influence over the judiciary and public media. In 2021, the Polish court ruled that some EU laws were incompatible with the Polish constitution. This was followed in turn by the EU claiming that Poland was a "direct challenge" to EU unity.

EU-skepticism is not confined to the government, as a small but growing number of Poles favor a Brexit-style "Polexit" break with the EU.

## To the Present

Poland continues to defy pessimists with its economic growth and stability, despite frequent political crises and ongoing issues with the EU. Warsaw has become a regional banking and finance hub with a skyline increasingly resembling that of Frankfurt or Canary Wharf.

This growth has not been without problems along the way. The political landscape has not mirrored the stability of the economy and the country is becoming increasingly polarized. The populist Law and Order (Prawo i Sprawiedliwość, or PiS) political party has been at the center of a number of extremely contentious decisions, among these the almost complete ban on abortions, which led to huge nation-wide street protests in 2020–21.

Poles showed overwhelming support for neighboring Ukraine following the Russian invasion in February 2022. Poland was by far the largest recipient of Ukrainian refugees fleeing the fighting, and ordinary Poles across the country opened their homes, volunteered, and donated money and much-needed items in support of their displaced neighbors. Unsurprisingly, historically Russophobic Poland was a world leader in calling for increased support for the Ukrainian war effort.

## ETHNIC GROUPS

For most of its history, Poland consisted of a mix of different ethnic groups, including Jews, Germans, Russians, Belarusians, and Ukrainians. Each has left its mark on Polish history and culture, but today the country is devoid of any sizable minority community.

At present, ethnic Poles make up 97 percent of the population, with Germans being the largest ethnic minority. The Jewish population of 3.5 million was almost entirely wiped out in the Holocaust. Most who survived emigrated to Israel or the United States. The shifting borders of the post-Second World War settlement resulted in the expulsion of 2 million Germans from Polish territory, while Poland's eastern fringe, which had largely been inhabited by Ukrainians, Belarusians, and

Lithuanians, became part of the Soviet Union. In the same period, some 3 million ethnic Poles were repatriated from the Soviet Union.

## THE INTELLIGENTSIA

The traditions of the landed gentry feature strongly in Polish folklore, and the descendants of these nobles are still extremely proud of their lineage. There exists a romantic image of nobles, often penniless, riding to and from each other's estates and enjoying the hospitality of their hosts. At the opposite end of the spectrum were the serfs, whose lot in life seems to have been overlooked by the folktales.

During the long period of foreign occupation, this landed upper class developed into what came to be known as the "intelligentsia," an educated elite. They led the Polish cultural and political resistance throughout the years of partition and established an unofficial government-in-exile in nineteenth-century Paris, keeping alive the dream of a proud, free Polish nation. With the return of independence at the end of the First World War, the intelligentsia helped guide the nation as the torchbearers of the culture and heritage of their ancestors.

The Second World War was disastrous for the intelligentsia; both the Soviets and the Nazis marked them out for deportation to labor camps or for execution in an attempt to deprive the country of its greatest source of inspiration and leadership.

The postwar Communist government was eager to educate young, working-class Poles from the countryside, resulting in a greatly altered background to the new intelligentsia. Some supported the socialist system, and others would eventually join with Solidarity to fight the government's strict control. In so doing, the latter group followed in the footsteps of their forefathers by keeping alive the idea of an independent, Western-looking Poland built on its traditional roots.

Since the fall of Communism, the intelligentsia has once again diversified and fragmented. The educated elite was for the most part economically protected under socialism. Today many intellectuals feel disenchanted and threatened by the impact of full-blooded capitalism, materialistic values, and consumerism. University professors working in the state system receive salaries that amount to a fraction of their Western European contemporaries, all of which has led to a new brain drain, mainly of scientists, to Western Europe and North America. This Polish upper class, much like the nation itself, seems to be at its strongest when its country, culture, and traditions are under threat.

## POLAND'S CITIES

### Warsaw

Poland's capital city is also the country's largest, with a population of approximately 1.8 million. Warsaw

Castle Square in Warsaw's lovingly reconstructed Old Town.

replaced Kraków as the Polish capital in 1596 due to its more central location in the Royal Republic of Poland–Lithuania that had been formed twenty-seven years earlier. Still centrally located within the country's post-Second World War borders, Warsaw lies on the Vistula River and is the heart of modern Poland's commercial sector.

The failed Warsaw Uprising against the Nazis in 1944 saw the historic core of the city reduced to rubble by the Germans. A massive postwar reconstruction project followed, as a result of which the charming Old Town was painstakingly restored to its original state and granted a place on UNESCO's World Heritage list. While the Old Town is an architectural gem, the rest of the city is a hodgepodge of styles ranging from

Skyscrapers flank the Soviet-era Palace of Culture and Science in central Warsaw.

original nineteenth-century palaces to row upon row of Communist-era residential blocks, to modern office towers that increasingly dominate the skyline.

Warsaw continues to expand, leading some to joke that it's a permanent construction site, but all "Varsovians" reap the benefits of the renovated and redesigned roads and infrastructure. Parks, laser and fountain shows, new libraries, museums, science centers, and a thriving restaurant scene all make it attractive to tourists and locals alike. Two metro lines, the second one still being extended, make commuting traffic-free and easy for 200 million passengers per year. The M1 metro line opened in 1995 and the M2 in 2015—the youngest metro system in Europe.

> ### *Vegan Varsovians*
>
> Despite the fact that traditional Polish cuisine is heavily based on meat dishes, most of the big cities love vegan restaurants. Warsaw has been named the sixth-most vegan-friendly city in the world by the Happy Cow website. Have you ever tried vegan *schabowy* (originally a pork cutlet) or kebab? Or vegan sushi and ramen? Well now you can, in Warsaw!

## Kraków

With a population of approximately 800,000, Kraków is Poland's second-largest city. It is situated on the banks of the Vistula River, 200 miles (322 km) south of Warsaw and just north of the Tatry Mountains.

Kraków's history dates back to the seventh century. The Catholic Church established itself in the city in the year 1000, and thirty-eight years later it became the Polish capital under the Piast Dynasty. Although Kraków has been invaded many times through the centuries it has remained relatively intact, and certainly fared better than Warsaw in the Second World War. The "cultural capital" of Poland is rich in historical sites, museums, and galleries. The Wawel Royal Castle and Wawel Hill constitute the most important historical and cultural site in the country. For centuries the residence of Poland's kings and the symbol of Polish statehood, the castle is now one of the country's premier art museums.

Wawel Royal Castle and Cathedral in Kraków.

Jagiełłonian University, founded in 1364, is still the most prestigious university in Poland. Although sometimes seen by residents of Warsaw as stuck-up and culturally conservative, Kraków is the place to experience traditional Polish culture and customs.

## Łódź

Until recently Poland's second-largest city (population 670,000), Łódź is centrally located, approximately 93 miles (150 km) southwest of Warsaw. The city is a product of the Industrial Revolution and built its wealth on textile factories, many of which were owned by Jews and Germans. The architecture consists largely of red-brick buildings mixed with the ubiquitous 1970s housing developments. Despite the fact that it used to be called "a promised land" and "a city of many cultures," Łódź has not benefited from the economic growth seen in other Polish cities and has suffered a mass exodus of inhabitants to Warsaw and Western Europe. It has, however, become popular with young artists. Łódź houses the legendary National Film School, whose alumni include the directors Krzysztof Kieślowski, Andrzej Wajda, and Roman Polański. There are numerous art exhibitions, workshops, and international exchange programs that attract artists and members of creative industries from all over the world, making Łódź a Polish artistic hub. It is also one of the world's greatest centers for urban street art, officially encouraging artists to enrich the cityscape with murals, graffiti, sculptures, installations, and "street jewelry."

## Wrocław

A city of 623,000 inhabitants, Wrocław is located on the Odra River in the southeast, just north of the Sudety Mountains and the Czech border. Wrocław, known to the Germans as Breslau, together with much of western Poland, was handed over to Poland in the post-Second World War settlement. Largely destroyed by the Russians as they drove westward into central Germany, today it bears little sign of this. Wrocław rivals Kraków in its majestic beauty, although the latter holds a truer place in the hearts of most Poles. Today it has one of the country's top universities and a vibrant youth culture.

Wyspa Piasek (Sand Island), one of several islands in the Odra River, Wrocław.

Wrocław was historically multicultural and shows the strong influences of German and Czech architecture and culture. Nowadays it is further enriched by the many international businesses that bring their employees to the region. After many of the coal mines and textile companies closed in the 1990s, the local economy deteriorated, leading to growing unemployment. To remedy the situation the local authorities created special economic zones and districts of economic activity around Wrocław and in the region of Lower Silesia specifically to attract tech and R&D companies. As a result, the economic situation in the region has improved significantly.

### City of Dwarves

Wrocław is also known as "the city of dwarves,"
as it boasts a collection of more than 350 tiny
statues of the mythological creatures hidden
all over town. The origins of this quirky
phenomenon are thought to lie in a satirical
reaction to the former PRL government's efforts
to censor anti-Communist slogans daubed by
activists. The activists would draw dwarves
over the splotches of red "censorship" paint; the
first was created in 1982. Currently, the city has
adopted the humble dwarf as its mascot, allowing
institutions, companies, and even individuals to
fund new dwarf statues. Each has a unique name
and history, and you can download a map to find
them all, or just go exploring and see how many
you can find yourself!

### Gdańsk

Gdańsk, the historically vital naval base on the Baltic and
the country's biggest trading port, has been strategically
important since the tenth century. The city has a
population of 470,000, which jumps to approximately
800,000 when the nearby cities of Sopot and Gdynia are
included (collectively known as the Tri-City). Gdańsk
has changed hands many times and has also held the
status of independent city-state. Owing to its strategic
military and commercial importance it has been much
fought over. From 1308 to 1454 it was part of the

The historic waterfront Crane Gate in Gdańsk.

monastic state of the Teutonic Knights, the unrelenting
enemies of the Poles  Hostilities came to a head in the
battle of Grunwald in 1410, later commemorated in
Nobel Prize-winner Henryk Sienkiewicz's novel *The
Knights of the Cross*. All this political turmoil has left
Gdańsk with a historic mix of Polish and German-style
buildings still standing in its Old Town.

The Second World War began in Gdańsk on
September 1, 1939, and it was the scene of the anti-
government demonstrations that led to the downfall
of Poland's Communist leader Władysław Gomułka in
December 1970. Ten years later its shipyards were the
birthplace of the Solidarity trade union movement,
whose opposition to the government helped topple
Communist Party rule in 1989. Gdańsk remains a
major port and industrial city, as well as a historical
site of culture.

Poznań

Located in western Poland, on the banks of the Warta River, Poznań (population 529,000) has existed since at least the ninth century and was home to Poland's first Christian king, Mieszko I, in the tenth century. The city has benefited from its location at the crossing of two crucial trading routes.

Poznan's golden age began in the sixteenth century. Not only was the city affluent, but it also became a center of learning, known throughout Europe. New universities and printing presses opened and the population doubled. Later years were marked by numerous wars (starting with Swedish Wars in 1703) and Prussian occupation. The resulting decline lasted until the end of the Second World War, by which time more than half of the city had been destroyed.

After the war, Poznań was aggressively industrialized and started to come alive again, reestablishing its historic traditions of education and industry. Nowadays Poznań continues to be transformed, implementing so-called "citizen friendly" policies and creating an "open city" mindset, accompanied by a significant growth in tourism. Famous landmarks include the Renaissance-style buildings in the Old Market Square and the Town Hall, which features a beautiful clock with mechanical goats that butt heads at the stroke of noon every day. Poznań is also famous for its beloved local pastry—a crescent roll with white poppy seed filling called St. Martin's croissant (Rogal Świętomarciński).

## A Tale of Two Capitals

"The big village" is how natives of Kraków describe Warsaw. They feel that the frenetic pace of life in the capital doesn't bear comparison with the more relaxed, cultured lifestyle of Kraków. For their part, most Warsaw residents hold no grudge against Kraków. They will openly admit that Warsaw cannot match its beauty or history, but don't take it seriously as a place where business can be done or careers made.

Both of these stereotypes are rooted in some degree of reality. First of all, Warsaw can at times feel like a village. In the aftermath of the Second World War, with the capital a virtual ghost town, the government encouraged villagers from the surrounding countryside to take up residence in the city. This new labor force was put to work in the massive task of reconstruction as well as in the new factories that were sprouting up. Even today, it can be difficult to find a resident of Warsaw who was born and raised in the city. In the last decades there has been an influx of young people in search of employment or a high standard of postsecondary education. Companies in Warsaw often prefer hiring such people over locals as their financial expectations are lower and they tend to be more amenable to working long hours.

As for Kraków, its residents still believe that they were robbed of their rightful status in 1596, when Zygmunt III moved the capital to Warsaw. It has certainly been left behind by the frantic pace of development set by Warsaw and attracts only a fraction of foreign investment in the country. Salaries are notably lower than in the capital, but so too is the cost of living. It has, however, retained its place as Poland's cultural capital. The sheer number of treasures in Kraków is unmatched by any other Polish city. Furthermore, the growth of international tourism has benefited Kraków far more than the capital, as anyone strolling through Kraków's Old Town can attest. And on a sunny afternoon, the sidewalk cafés on its main square easily outshine Warsaw's crowded bars.

### *"Jars"*

Born and bred Varsovians are often not terribly fond of those who have moved to the capital from the countryside. These newcomers are sometimes jokingly referred to as "Jars," as they visit their hometowns and villages during holidays and long weekends, returning with jars of homemade delicacies from worried mothers, grandmothers, and aunts.

## GOVERNMENT AND POLITICS

Since the first free elections were held on October 27, 1991, the Republic of Poland has been a parliamentary democracy with a structure very similar to that of many other European Union countries. The current workings of the government and presidency were set out in the Easter Constitution of October 1997.

## The Presidency

The new constitution weakened the role of the president but left intact certain executive powers. The president is commander-in-chief of the armed forces, has influence in appointing military and foreign policy officials, and can veto any bill, although this veto can be overruled by a three-fifths majority in parliament.

Former Solidarity leader Lech Wałęsa won the first free presidential election, but quickly fell out of favor when he proved less competent in office than he had been in opposing the Communists. After being narrowly defeated by Aleksander Kwaśniewski in 1995, he was humiliated by the incumbent five years later when he gained only 1.43 percent of the vote. Many Poles still regard Wałęsa with gratitude and fondness but wish he had stepped out of the spotlight once the changes he had fought for had come into effect. During his ten years in power, Kwaśniewski pursued closer ties with NATO and the EU, eventually securing Poland's membership in both—NATO in 1999 and the EU in 2004.

Kwaśniewski's successor was the controversial far-right Law and Justice Party (PiS) leader Lech Kaczyński. A staunch anti-Communist, he promised, among other things, a return to traditional Catholic Polish values. During his time as mayor of Warsaw, a position he'd held for five years prior to his successful presidential bid, he banned Gay Pride parades and sanctioned a right-wing youth group's "Parade of Normality" in its place.

In 2010, a Russian-made Tupolev aircraft carrying the president, his wife, and a number of high-ranking military officials crashed on the approach to Smolensk air force base in Russia. There were no survivors. Great significance was placed on the fact that the trip had been undertaken to commemorate the seventieth anniversary of the Katyn massacre, in which more than 20,000 Polish officers were murdered by the Soviets. Many Kaczyński supporters still believe conspiracy theories that the plane was brought down intentionally by the Russians, despite the fact that no evidence to support these theories was ever found.

Lech Kaczyński's twin brother Jarosław served as the leader of the Law and Justice Party from 2003 and as prime minister in 2006–2007. Following the president's death, the Speaker of the Parliament, Bronisław Komorowski, from the Civic Platform Party, served as temporary head of state for three months, and later won the election against Jarosław Kaczyński, becoming Poland's next left-leaning president.

Andrzej Duda of Kaczyński's PiS Party won the next presidential election in 2015, and a majority of seats in the parliament. Despite not serving as prime minister since 2007, Jarosław Kaczyński is still considered the most influential politician in the country. His political goal is to take Poland back to its conservative, Roman Catholic roots and away from the multicultural Western European mainstream. He is a Euroskeptic, regarding Western liberal values as an existential threat to Poland and Polish culture. His conservative values and anti-Western stance have won him support from many elderly and economically marginalized Poles, who have largely been excluded from the benefits of EU membership and the increasingly digital infrastructure.

Having no party-political affiliation is increasingly becoming an asset in Poland. By and large, the Poles have become disillusioned with the reform process and much of the enthusiasm of the 1990s and early 2000s has been replaced by indifference and skepticism. The loss of faith in both leading political parties, combined with the emergence of more radical parties, has left many younger Poles feeling they have no one who represents their views, and that they are powerless against the establishment.

## The Parliament

The Polish parliament is made up of two chambers: the Sejm, which has 460 members elected by proportional representation, and the Senate, made up of 100 senators, elected by a majority voting system. Unlike the presidency, which has a five-year term, both the Sejm and Senate are elected for four years. The minimum percentage of votes required for representation in the Sejm is 5 percent for individual parties and 8 percent for multiparty coalitions. Exceptions to this rule are made for special-interest minority groups such as the ethnic German minority.

The position of prime minister has been a much less stable one than that of the president. Political parties are volatile as well. Although the same faces seem to stay in circulation, the parties and coalitions change frequently.

## POLAND IN THE EUROPEAN UNION

The long process of Poland's integration into the European Union brought to the surface many of the deep feelings and insecurities that Poles have about their place in Europe. They regard themselves as very much belonging to a Europe that predates the EU. They see their history, both the good and the bad, as being inexorably linked with that of Western Europe. While many Western Europeans think of the natural boundaries of Western Europe as being defined by the German–Polish border, many Poles see it lying on Poland's eastern border with Belarus and Ukraine.

EU membership is seen as a right, and many were frustrated when Brussels and the founder states expected Poland to consider it a privilege. This point of view is deeply entrenched and Poles react very negatively to being told what to do by the "West." Since Poland's accession to the EU in 2004 the two sides have slowly grown apart. Poland is increasingly seen in the rest of Europe as a fundamental part of the Union, but the famous Polish inferiority complex regarding the West seems to be alive and well, despite a renewed self-confidence supported by the continuing growth of the economy.

Despite their anti-EU sentiments, a significant majority of Poles still support continued membership of the EU. Poland is also one of the largest monetary beneficiaries of EU membership, having received more than €17 billion in funding for investment in motorways, roads, public transportation, and redeveloping cities and towns across the country.

In 2014, when the PiS Party came into power, the European Commission published the first of many "rule-of-law" assessments criticizing the Polish courts, judiciary reforms, and public media law. In October 2021, the European Court of Justice fined Poland €1 million per day for breaking EU law by failing to close down the disciplinary chamber of its Supreme Court. The fine is the highest penalty imposed on any EU member state.

### Post–EU Emigration

Poland was fortunate to join the European Union before the global financial crisis, which brought with it widespread restrictions on the freedom of movement for citizens of new member states. Although no official records exist, it has been estimated that up to two million Poles have emigrated since the country joined the EU in 2004. Approximately half of those moved to the UK. Emigrants are often young, educated, and speak foreign languages, while the jobs they undertake abroad are often low-skilled positions. Another sizable group leaving the country are highly educated and highly skilled Poles, often in the medical profession, IT, or engineering. All of Poland has been affected by this brain drain of young, highly skilled workers. Most Poles now have close friends or family working in "the West."

# CHAPTER TWO

# VALUES &
# ATTITUDES

Over the centuries Polish culture has been shaped by many factors. The defining presence of the Catholic Church, generations of proud nobles, great city centers of trade and learning, ever-shifting borders, numerous wars, foreign occupation, and Communism have all left their mark.

## CATHOLICISM IN POLAND

Throughout the Communist period the Catholic Church was the only large-scale organization outside Party control. The Church organized extracurricular religious lessons for school children, which most children attended. Increasingly, membership of the Church became synonymous with being against the political establishment. This was demonstrated by Pope John Paul II's first homecoming as pope in 1979, in which more than a hundred thousand turned out for an open-air Mass in Warsaw. The Pope, a staunch

Pope John Paul II's rapturous reception in Poland in 1979.

anti-Communist, inspired the Solidarity Trade Union in its struggle and the trade union, in turn, became increasingly attached to conservative Catholic values.

Western European visitors to Poland may be surprised to see how strong a role the Church continues to play in the day-to-day lives of many Polish people. Furthermore, the strength of this appeal can be seen across the demographic spectrum, with young and old, wealthy and impoverished, educated and unskilled, all congregating on Sunday mornings and throughout the week. Even the many who do not attend Mass are strongly influenced by the culture of Polish Catholicism.

Mass during the annual harvest festival of Dozynki in Rogow village.

In recent years, however, the Church has been declining in popularity, especially among the younger generation. Fewer parents are signing their children up for religion classes in school, fewer young people are going to church, and the diminishing number of candidates applying to seminaries has led the Vatican to shut down almost twenty of these colleges.

Although young people are turning away from the Church as an institution, many retain their belief. Their disillusionment is often blamed on the political ties between the Church and certain political groups. Others attribute it to the very conservative values of the Polish Catholic Church and its unwillingness to change with the times. Its immovable stance on issues such as contraception and abortion, as well as the blind eye it has turned to the abuse of children by priests, are examples of this.

### Sunday Observance

A foreigner in his first year living in Poland was quite surprised at being told off by the elderly lady in the apartment next door for using his washing machine on a Sunday. Years later, in a detached house and now safe to use the washing machine whenever he fancied, he was told off by the next-door neighbor—a computer specialist in his twenties—for mowing the lawn on a Sunday!

In 2020–21, in the middle of the Covid-19 pandemic, mass "Women's Strike" protests took place in Poland after the ruling PiS Party tightened the law on abortion, making almost all cases of abortion illegal. Despite the fact that the majority of Poles opposed the changes, the Roman Catholic Church praised the new legislation, resulting in a backlash against its political interference. The Women's Strike protests made international headlines and were the biggest anti-government demonstrations in Poland since the anti-Communist protests of 1989.

It is difficult to distinguish between religion and national culture in Poland as the two have become so intertwined. Behavior that a visitor might initially attribute to deep religious conviction may in fact be simply an expression of Polish cultural norms. Religious celebrations are a perfect example of this. Over Easter and Christmas the churches are bursting at the seams, the streets empty, and after Mass everyone rushes back to the family home for a traditional home-cooked meal washed down by a few shots of vodka. However, many of those participating in these festivities openly admit that they are not devout believers. Religious types maintain that Polish culture is Catholic culture, but young people largely disagree. Nowadays, while most people do enjoy the family gatherings and traditional Christmas and Easter fare, they skip the churchgoing part and treat the occasion as an opportunity to catch up with family and have a relaxing long weekend.

## PRIDE AND PATRIOTISM

Poland has had more than its fair share of foreign domination and war. That the Polish nation has come through this in the state it is today—a modern, increasingly prosperous, Western economy—is a source of pride for Poles. However, Polish attitudes toward their state or nation are complex and may seem contradictory to foreigners. The contradiction lies in the Polish tendency to mock their country and laugh at themselves, much as the British would, while at the same time having a straightforward, American-style

Hanging out the national flag on May 3, Constitution Day.

pride in it. After the years of mismanagement during the Communist era, government and politicians in general remain natural objects of ridicule. But the Polish nation itself is viewed as something sacred, not to be criticized or joked about.

Thus, while Poles may laugh about their plight, the state of their country, or typical Polish characteristics, foreigners should not do the same. The Poles are extremely sensitive to foreign opinions of their country and themselves. It is not at all uncommon to see Polish flags flying from shop fronts and outside apartment windows on national holidays such as Constitution Day and Independence Day. Nor is it unusual to hear the national anthem actually being sung proudly by all in attendance at sporting events and official gatherings.

In recent years, Polish Independence Day, celebrated on November 11, has been largely hijacked by right-wing nationalists holding marches and voicing their populist views on issues such as immigration and LGBTQ+ rights.

### *Local Heroes*

Any Pole who gains international sporting recognition and success is certain to be loved at home. Relatively obscure sports quickly become national obsessions the moment a Pole becomes a top-flight contender. Examples of this include former ski jumper Adam Małysz; former Formula 1 driver Robert Kubica; cyclist Michał Kwiatkowski; and both the men's and women's world-championship-winning volleyball teams. More recent sporting stars include the Barcelona striker Robert Lewandowski and tennis player Iga Świątek (ranked world no. 1 by the Women's Tennis Association in 2022).

The Poles are also extremely proud of their historical figures. They include such luminaries as Mikołaj Kopernik, Maria Skłodowska-Curie, Pope John Paul II, Adam Mickiewicz, and Fryderyk Chopin.

## ATTITUDES TOWARD RULES:
## IS ANYONE WATCHING?

A common stereotype of the Germans is that even when driving in a forest, with no other cars for miles, they will still signal before turning. The stereotypical Polish driver, on the other hand, can be in the middle of the busy city yet won't signal unless there is another car in the immediate vicinity. Everyone speeds—if you follow the rules, you're slowing everyone else down.

In Poland, rules are not sacred—they can often be bent or made to fit different situations. From a foreign perspective, the Polish attitude toward rules can seem to be a contradictory combination of conformity and anarchy. Complex attitudes were a necessary survival technique in Communist times. Without breaking any regulations it was almost impossible to procure sought-after goods such as Western blue jeans or highly rationed foodstuffs or alcohol. Other regulations, mostly political, were untouchable, however, and these were rarely tampered with. In other words, rules were bent or broken when doing so was without consequence.

All this can have a confusing effect on foreigners who are unfamiliar with the "rules of the game." In the office, for example, rules that are clearly explained and whose purpose is understood are far more likely to be followed by employees than regulations that are simply stated in an impersonal manner and subsequently left unmonitored.

Today, many Poles feel frustrated by the general disregard for rules in society. Although this attitude seems to allow more individual freedom, it leads to uncertainty about how to behave in certain places and situations, as well as to a lack of respect for public property and spaces. During Communist times it was popular to say of public spaces, "It belongs to everyone, therefore it belongs to no one," and so most people felt no responsibility to pick up litter or criticize vandals. Many Poles who have traveled abroad wish that Poland was more orderly, like Switzerland or Japan, but attitudes change slowly.

### Kombinować

The Poles even have a word to proudly proclaim that they have managed to acquire goods or services by stretching or ignoring the rules. *Kombinować*, which translates as combine, or contrive, is often related to the Communist period when little could be done or obtained without officially documented permission. Times may have changed, but the mindset partially remains. Today, *kombinować* means to use your brains to come up with a shortcut or an innovative solution rather than relying on a collective approach and set rules.

## BRIBERY AND CORRUPTION

In the past, irksome regulations were often circumvented with a bribe. Although the daily papers are full of stories of corruption at the highest levels of government and industry, such practices are increasingly on the decline and regarded as unacceptable. The very fact that corruption is investigated with such zeal is a positive change. Everyday corruption, or the giving of "presents," is still quite common, but it is best for foreigners not to make such offers as the whole process is very delicate and offering the wrong gift to the wrong person can cause great offense. Having said that, there is a fine line between showing gratitude and bribery. Giving small presents to someone who has offered genuine assistance is becoming less common, as providing a service is seen as part of their job. Most companies and universities have implemented an open-door policy, meaning that no meeting is held behind closed doors to avoid claims of unfair treatment, harassment, or bribery.

## CHIVALRY OR SEXISM?

The fact that political correctness has never really caught on in Poland to the extent that it has in the West can be a breath of fresh air for visitors, but at the same time certain situations can prove awkward. This is perhaps most evident in the attitudes of older Polish men toward women. On the face of it, Polish men are perfect gentlemen—walking on the street side of the sidewalk when accompanying a woman, holding doors open, and offering seats on trams and buses.

While it is not at all unusual for Polish women to have their own careers—and in certain professions, such as medicine and the law, they are well represented—it is much less common to see women in top management positions in large companies. A glass ceiling definitely exists in many Polish companies, above which women have great difficulty progressing. Additionally, it can be difficult for a young, recently married woman to find employment in a private company owing to the employer's fear of having to pay for maternity leave. Technically, it is illegal for employers to discriminate on this basis, but in reality there is almost nothing a woman can do in such a situation, especially in small firms. Most state-owned and international companies implement their own fair treatment policies, and both maternity and paternity leave, as well as other benefits, are available to help staff maintain their work–life balance.

Once again, the importance of the generation gap should be stressed. Among young people attitudes toward women are much more progressive and women are far less likely to find themselves in awkward or difficult situations. There is still much to be done, though, as Poland currently ranks thirtieth worldwide according to the SDG Gender Index.

## ATTITUDES TOWARD MONEY

Attitudes toward money differ very little between Poland and Western European countries, but there are some points to be aware of. First of all, "how much" questions should be avoided in normal conversation, whether in regard to someone's new computer or, of course, salaries. Also, many things in Poland, such as a night out, are still cheaper than in Western Europe.

After decades of limited opportunities to buy imported goods, many Poles now spend a large portion of their salaries on new cars, designer clothes, and electronic gadgets. In Warsaw in particular, the visitor may be surprised by the number of luxury cars. Among businesspeople it is most unlikely that anyone in a high position would not have the appropriate class of car. Furthermore, those who own such status symbols are always eager to talk about them, while those who don't will often go into detail describing why they haven't yet got one, but plan to in the future.

Overall, prices in Poland have gradually grown closer to those in Western Europe, yet salaries are significantly lower. Low incomes and the high cost of living are increasingly problematic, and the Poles are not shy about voicing these concerns.

## ATTITUDES TOWARD FOREIGNERS

One of the visible changes since Communist times has been the influx of tourists, foreign students, and expatriates, especially in the large cities. The curiosity that locals used to show at a foreigner in their city has all but gone, although the sound of English in smaller towns and villages can still attract interest. Foreigners can, for the most part, expect a warm welcome.

As with all places, however, the warmth of the welcome may depend on where one comes from. "Westerners," especially native English speakers, are the lucky ones. First of all, English is very popular and most young people in the cities speak a little at least. Secondly, Poles in general are fond of the English and Americans, and very curious about Canadians, Australians, and New Zealanders. In fact, during the gray days of Communist rule, Canada was synonymous with paradise in colloquial Polish.

At the opposite end of the spectrum tend to be visitors from countries of the former Soviet Union. This is largely the result of the unpleasant history between Poland and Russia. In recent years there has been an influx of migrants from Eastern Europe and Central Asia. While Poland has experienced a huge brain drain to the West, it is now not at all uncommon to see Ukrainians, Belarusians, and Kazakhs working as drivers, nurses, or shop assistants.

Recent tensions between Russia and some of its neighbors, Ukraine in particular, have had the effect of strengthening the bonds Poles feel with these countries. Many ethnic Poles live in former Soviet republics, largely as a result of Stalin's spatial redistribution of ethnic communities following the Second World War. In 2022, more than 6 million refugees from Ukraine, mostly women and children, crossed the Polish border and were granted special privileges, including access to free education and medical care, welfare benefits, and even free public transportation for a limited time. In addition to government support, many ordinary citizens volunteered their time to collect food, clothing, and money for Ukrainians fleeing the war. Others offered refugees accommodation in their homes.

## RACISM AND HOMOPHOBIA

Happily, in recent years racism has declined markedly. Mixed marriages have become more common and schools have increasing numbers of mixed-race pupils.

While racial discrimination is slowly becoming less common, homophobia is still rife. Members of the LGBTQ+ community are still discriminated against and vilified, especially in the state-owned national media. Same-sex marriage is not legal in Poland and

At the equality march on Kraków's Gay Pride Parade in 2022.

generally LGBTQ+ Poles are forced to keep their identities secret.

## THE GENERATION GAP

It is a truism that values and attitudes vary from generation to generation. In the former Communist countries of Central and Eastern Europe, however, this is particularly marked. The economic changes that have taken place in Poland since 1989 have been fruitful for many but have largely left the older generation behind.

The average age of managers and directors in Poland is much younger than in Western Europe, as it was often easier for companies to train young people than to retrain those aging managers accustomed to the state-run monopolies of the past. Young professionals have far more opportunities than their more experienced elders, and are therefore in a better financial situation.

Educated young professionals tend to have much more open, liberal attitudes compared to the conservative, Catholic values of their parents. The young embrace new fashions and trends, while their parents tend to have more traditional lifestyles. Pubs, cafés, and restaurants are very popular with young, urban Poles; the older generation prefers to entertain at home.

## THE URBAN–RURAL GAP

While most urban centers have witnessed rejuvenation and growth in the years since the collapse of Communism, the small towns and villages have suffered. The vast majority of direct foreign investment goes into the large cities, primarily Warsaw, Kraków, and Poznań. The countryside has seen little or none of this, and those in the agricultural sector have been hardest hit by the economic changes.

Despite intensive urbanization during the 1940s and '50s, farming still employs more than 2 million Poles. Under the EU's Common Agricultural Policy (CAP), which contributes more than 2 billion euros annually to the Polish agricultural sector, the economic situation for Polish farmers has improved significantly. Notwithstanding the EU subsidies available to improve the situation in the countryside, the biggest problems for people in rural areas remain low incomes, difficult access to schools and hospitals, and lower life satisfaction.

### The Polish Countryside

Polish farms have traditionally been divided among siblings over the generations, resulting in ever more numerous, but ever smaller, farms. When flying over Germany into Poland the change is immediately apparent as the large tracts of land give way to the tiny, irregular plots that typify the Polish agricultural landscape. The fact that farms remained privately owned in Poland during Communism seemed at the time to be a victory for Polish farmers, but the small size of these enterprises makes them uncompetitive with the massive, technologically advanced food industry of Western Europe. Polish agriculture is changing, however, albeit slowly. EU funding, technological advances, and the migration of young people from rural to urban areas have all resulted in the increasing efficiency of the agricultural sector.

## THE LEGACY OF COMMUNISM

The effects of forty years of state socialism on Polish values and attitudes are still very evident, and not only among the generations that grew up in the Communist system but in the younger generation as well.

Perhaps the strongest impact has been on the work ethic. Most Poles never really believed the socialist propaganda and working for the state (as the vast majority did) increasingly became thought of as working for an illegitimate power. As this "us versus them" atmosphere intensified, there seemed less and less logic in doing your job well, especially given the wasteful overemployment of the system. Stealing from the workplace was common, with the excuse "The property of the state belongs to everyone, so why not take home what is partly mine."

Another manifestation of this legacy is in attitudes toward authority. Anyone, from a policeman to a train conductor, who had authority over people was viewed with suspicion, and elaborate systems were developed to "beat the system." Although this mentality is changing, negative attitudes to those in authority are still evident and foreign managers working in Poland often note the anti-authoritarian attitudes of their staff.

# CHAPTER THREE

# CUSTOMS &
# TRADITIONS

Few can compete with the Poles when it comes to enthusiastic celebration. This is as true for religious and public holidays as it is for special occasions such as weddings and name days. Moreover, many Polish customs and ways of celebrating traditional Catholic holidays have a strong pagan element, giving them a distinctive flavor.

During the decades of Communism there were very few affordable venues such as restaurants or pubs and Poles became masters of entertaining at home. This also reflects the long tradition of the Polish nobility, who were famous for their hospitality and grand feasts. The Poles say "A guest in the home is God in the home," and despite the fact that Polish cities are no longer devoid of restaurants and public houses, the custom of entertaining at home is still very much alive. When invited to celebrate a holiday or special occasion with a Polish family, the foreigner is in for a treat and should be prepared for a grand feast and a late night.

## PUBLIC HOLIDAYS

**January 1**  New Year's Day

**January 6**  Epiphany (Three King's Day)

**March/April (movable)**  Easter Sunday and Monday

**May 1**  Labor Day

**May 3**  Constitution Day

**June (movable)**  Corpus Christi

**August 15**  Feast of the Assumption / Armed Forces Day

**November 1**  All Saints' Day

**November 11**  Independence Day

**December 25**  Christmas Day

**December 26**  Boxing Day

## HOLIDAYS AND EVENTS

### Carnival

Carnival in Warsaw or Kraków may not be as glamorous as in Rio de Janeiro or Venice but it has its own charm. The first signs of Carnival are the crowds at discos and pubs. Young people in particular enjoy the carnival atmosphere as a break from the dreariness of winter, work, or upcoming exams. Those who have outgrown the disco usually organize home parties throughout the period from New Year to the beginning of Lent—the forty days of fasting that start on Ash Wednesday and last till Easter Sunday.

In the mountains and the countryside, Poles celebrate Carnival outdoors with a traditional bonfire and sleigh ride (*kulig*), while drinking plenty of mulled beer or wine to keep warm.

The last Thursday before Lent is known as Fat Thursday (Tłusty Czwartek). It is the day when the lines outside delicatessens and sweet shops can stretch around city blocks as the whole country gorges on traditional sweet, heavy doughnuts (*pączki*) before, theoretically at least, having to give up such delicacies for Lent. The final Tuesday of Carnival (Ostatki) represents the last chance for strict Catholics to enjoy loud music, dancing, alcohol, meat, and sweets before the Lenten fast.

Even those who don't consider themselves religious often respect the days of Lent, refraining from going to parties and avoiding conspicuous consumption. Many people simply see the period as an opportunity to rein in their bad habits. As such, it's a popular time for Poles to go on a diet, cut down on drinking, exercise more regularly, or simply live a healthier life for a few weeks.

## Easter

The Easter holiday equals Christmas for tradition and importance in Poland, although Western-style consumerism in recent years has given Christmas a glitzier appearance.

Lent culminates in "Holy Week" (Wielki Tydzień), beginning with Palm Sunday. Due to the lack of subtropical palms in Central Europe, Poles use pussy willows and sticks with special floral arrangements in their place. On Palm Sunday these floral arrangements are blessed in the local church and carried through the streets by parishioners in a procession led by the priest.

Good Friday (Wielki Piątek) in Poland is not a public holiday. It is, nonetheless, an important day for the faithful, and one spent in stark contrast to the joyous atmosphere of the rest of Holy Week. Good Friday Mass is a somber occasion as worshipers reflect on the death of Christ. After Mass in many parishes a cross is carried in procession; in others there are visits to models of the Holy Sepulcher. Back at home, meanwhile, preparations will be well under way for the Easter Sunday feast.

On Holy Saturday (Wielka Sobota), families prepare small, elaborately decorated wicker baskets containing

*Mazurek* pastry, a traditional Polish Easter dessert made of shortcrust pastry, chocolate cream, candied fruit, nuts, and almonds.

portions of the food to be served on Easter Sunday. Typically these are a boiled egg, a piece of sausage, bread, salt, pepper, and the figure of a lamb (the symbol of Easter) made of sugar. Each basket is sprinkled with holy water and blessed by the priest after Mass.

The fasting of Lent finally ends after morning Mass on Easter Sunday, when feasting begins with a massive breakfast. In many homes the feasting continues more or less uninterrupted throughout the day with a variety of traditional dishes washed down with wine or vodka. The festive atmosphere, the abundance of food and drink, and the lighting of firecrackers outside are a complete contrast to the peace and quiet of Lent.

## Śmigus-Dyngus

Those who do not like getting wet had best not visit Poland on Easter Monday, better known as Śmigus-dyngus. In a "fun" tradition with clear pagan origins and connected with the coming of spring, young men roam the streets searching for victims to be drenched with water. Traditionally it was unmarried girls who were doused, but today it could be anyone with the misfortune of turning down the wrong street.

## The First Week of May

The first week of May is a time to escape for a spring break, as both May 1 and 3 are public holidays. May 1 is Labor Day and no longer holds any special significance in post-Communist Poland. The anniversary of the signing of Poland's first written constitution in 1791 is celebrated on May 3. Official ceremonies and parades take place and patriots fly flags from their windows, but for the most part the significance of the day is lost on the vacationing crowds. Many offices even close down altogether for the week and the cities empty as people head out in search of spring sunshine.

### Corpus Christi

Those who enjoy folk costumes shouldn't miss the traditional Corpus Christi processions on the first Thursday after Trinity Sunday. The town of Łowicz, to the west of Warsaw, in particular is known for its colorful yet solemn celebrations.

People wearing traditional folk costume from the Łowicz region during Corpus Christi.

## All Saints' Day—All Souls' Day

The most solemn of the traditional holidays, All Saints'
Day and All Souls' Day, on November 1 and 2, are
devoted to remembering the dead and most people
spend these days visiting the graves of family members.

Only the first of the two days is a national holiday.
The second day is dedicated to praying for the souls
of the departed. Relatives visit the cemetery, clean
around the graves, and, most importantly, light votive
candles and leave flowers such as chrysanthemums. The
cemeteries at night have a surreal air with the warm
glow of thousands of candles.

There are pagan elements mixed in with the religious
devotions of All Saints' Day. There used to be, and still is
to some degree, a belief that the spirits of the dead were
free to roam on this day, and food was left at the graves
to appease them.

Since All Saints' Day is such a solemn occasion, many
pius Poles frown at the idea of Halloween. It is seen by
some as garish and inappropriate, and trick-or-treaters
may even be yelled at when knocking on doors in search
of candies.

## St. Andrew's Day

Another day with a mixture of Catholic and pagan
traditions is St. Andrew's Day (Andrzejki), just after the
fall equinox on November 30. Although not a national
holiday, many people celebrate it by attending parties
in honor of those named Andrzej (Andrew). Children
celebrate it by, among other things, pouring melted wax
through the hole of a key into a bucket of water. The

hardened pieces of wax are then held in front of a light, and the shadow cast against the wall is said to predict what the coming year will bring.

## St. Nicholas's Day
The Christmas festivities actually begin on St. Nicholas' Day (Mikołajki), December 6. Traditionally an adult would dress up in a long robe, resembling a bishop more than the Western Santa Claus, and distribute presents and candies to the good children and sticks to the naughty ones. Nowadays, parents put small gifts under the pillows of sleeping children (or in their shoes in some regions) so that upon waking they find a surprise from St. Nicholas.

## Christmas (Boże Narodzenie)
This is a very special time for Poles. In no other holiday are national customs and traditions kept alive as faithfully as at Christmas. The most important day of the period is Christmas Eve (Wigilia). Although it is not an official holiday, most people either take the day off or leave work early as the festivities are meant to begin once the first star has been sighted.

The traditional Wigilia dinner is very specific, consisting of twelve courses, none with meat. Carp, herring, and dumplings (*pierogi*) stuffed with sauerkraut and mushrooms, and poppy seed cakes are some of the most popular dishes. An extra place is set at the table for an unexpected guest or the spirits of ancestors who are said to be present on this night. Hay is placed under a white tablecloth to represent the stable in which Jesus was born, and pieces of hay pulled from under the tablecloth can be

Christmas fair in the Old Town of Gdańsk at night.

used to predict one's future. During the feast presents are exchanged, all supposedly from St. Nicholas. After the meal, the faithful make their way to midnight Mass, after which meat may once again be eaten.

Wigilia, like other Christian celebrations in Poland, has retained many superstitious elements that add a special flavor to the evening. Among these is the belief that animals can speak at midnight. As everyone should be at Mass, however, there is no one to hear them. Various traditional methods of fortune telling are also employed, mostly to determine the fate of any unmarried girls or predict the size of the harvest in the coming year. Many of these superstitions are remnants of pagan midwinter celebrations.

December 25 is generally spent quietly with the family. Christmas Day is the first of the twelve days of Christmas. The feasting continues on this day with *bigos*, or the traditional hunters' stew.

St. Stephen's Day (December 26) is an opportunity to visit friends and family or see the elaborate Christmas displays in churches. As well as nativity scenes, these may include colorful castles made of tin paper, and miniature mechanized villages with moving figures and trains.

## New Year's Eve

New Year's Eve is yet another opportunity for a party. In Warsaw in particular, formal balls have become very fashionable with young and old alike. Entertaining at home is widespread with, in typical Polish style, a grand feast and plenty of vodka and champagne. Also popular are the outdoor events organized by most towns and cities, sponsored by TV or radio stations. These are often hosted by B-list celebrities and include a line-up of performers singing the year's biggest hits. These events are usually held in town squares and the biggest ones in the country are televised and streamed live online. In Warsaw the NYE countdown concert is held in Constitution Square in the city center. If you plan on attending, bring your own booze (even though drinking alcohol in public is illegal, police let it slide this one night) and bundle up as the temperatures sometimes drop to -15° Celsius. Not that the weather stops revelers from staying long into the small hours.

## SPECIAL OCCASIONS

## Name Days

Birthdays celebrations are mostly held for children. Name days on the other hand are celebrated in style.

Practically all Poles have traditional Christian first names, and each name matches a day when that particular saint is honored. For example, anyone named Andrzej (Andrew) will celebrate his name day on St. Andrew's Day, November 30.

Unlike birthdays, there is no need for the person celebrating to tell others their age. Additionally, everyone knows by a simple glance at the calendar when someone has their name day. The person celebrating normally organizes a small party for family and friends. A separate small celebration may be held at work, with colleagues taking a break from their duties to sing the traditional "*Sto Lat*"—"(Live) one hundred years"—and enjoy some cake and candies.

## Weddings

Polish wedding parties are famous for their intensity and duration. Even families with modest incomes will do everything in their power to ensure that their guests are well taken care of. A typical wedding party will end the next morning, with accommodation often provided for closest friends and family. Weddings in the southern Tatry Mountain region are famous for lasting an entire week! In many parts of the country, including the Tatry, it is not unusual for the guests to attend in traditional folk costumes. If you are invited to a wedding, it is customary to give an envelope with money as a gift. Money is the safest gift, as the newlyweds can either use it to help cover the wedding costs or put it toward their new life together.

# CHAPTER FOUR

# MAKING FRIENDS

The Poles are outgoing, gregarious people. However, on first meeting a stranger, especially without a personal introduction from a mutual acquaintance, they are often guarded and distant. They feel little need to go out of their way to be excessively polite to someone whom they know nothing about. Poles consider excessive politeness to strangers to be unnatural, insincere, and a little embarrassing. Such attitudes to strangers are in stark contrast to the warm welcome they reserve for friends and relatives.

## MEETING THE POLES

A first-time visitor to Poland may well come to believe that, in terms of friendliness and formality, there are only two extremes. Poles seem to be either very friendly or cold and distant. In fact, the form of behavior depends on the context of the encounter. North Americans in particular, who are generally open and relatively informal with most people they meet, may find these social rules difficult to cope with. Americans may refer to anyone they have good relations with as a "friend." Poles reserve this word for people with whom they have a very close bond, usually forged over many years.

### Friends in the Right Places

Personal relationships are very important and complex in Polish society. As we've seen, informal personal networks were crucial during the period of state socialism, when it was practically impossible to do anything outside the strict regulations without "a friend in the right place." Although they are no longer a necessity, such networks have evolved and still play an important social role. A Polish friend will always be happy to introduce you to a friend of theirs if it can help with a particular problem.

As personal contacts are so important in Poland, the easiest way to meet people and strike up a friendship is through a mutual friend. The fact that a third party introduces you as a friend means that you can be trusted. Furthermore, you will generally be accepted as a friend after such an introduction. Without this assurance by a third party, Poles can at times seem cold and suspicious when meeting people for the first time.

If you are contacting someone whose name you have been given by a mutual acquaintance, be sure to mention this at the outset as it will make the conversation much easier.

## FORMAL AND INFORMAL FORMS
## OF ADDRESS

The appropriate degree of formality is a complex matter and has more to do with the relative status of individuals than it does with how they were introduced.

### Hey You!

A difficult aspect of Polish conversation for foreigners is the seemingly simple distinction between "*Pan/Pani*" (Sir/Madam) and "*ty*" (you). Linguistically, such a distinction is common in many languages, but its social implications are extremely important in Poland. The bad news is that using the wrong form of address can be a faux pas equivalent to calling your spouse by your lover's name. The good news is that foreigners are generally excused such mistakes.

Don't be surprised, when first meeting a Pole, if they become awkward every time they have to use the word "you" in English. In Polish, a simple question such as "Where do you come from?" has the construction "Where does Sir/Madam come from?" This very formal form of address is especially important when speaking to an elderly person or, in business, one's superior. This situation is normally ended when the senior person proposes they call each other by the much less formal "*ty*."

Poles who are fluent in English and more experienced in dealing with foreigners will not struggle with "you," but the social implications of this are far-reaching. Many foreign managers find that there is a huge gulf in Poland between formal and informal behavior. For example, it is not very common in Poland to be on first-name terms with one's boss. Even if the boss is open to being on first-name terms, employees will most likely address them as Mr./Ms. followed by their first name. Relationships among peers, however, can change very quickly from being extremely formal to being the slap-on-the-back "best friends" variety. Americans may be comfortable with the latter, but Western Europeans tend to be used to something in between.

### *"Have We Been Introduced?"*

When Starbucks opened in Poland in 2009, baristas were trained to serve customers in the American manner—big smiles, friendly attitude, and addressing everyone with the informal "*ty*" (you). And, of course, they asked for the customer's first name, which would later be called when their coffee was ready. For many Poles, to be greeted as a close friend by some teenage member of staff was simply scandalous, and would sometimes elicit the response of "Since when are we on first-name terms?" There were even opinion pieces in the newspapers lamenting the loss of proper manners! After a while, people grew accustomed to this overfamiliarity and it is now increasingly common for staff in trendy cafés to address all customers in a direct and informal manner.

The best way to deal with this rather complicated situation is to say something like "Please, call me John" when constantly being referred to as Mr. Doe. Finally, make sure to address the person you are speaking to in the same way that they address you. Which means that if he's referring to you as "Mr. Smith," you may well be stuck with "Mr. Brzęczyszczykiewicz."

## Conversation

Poles are generally easy to talk to and it is usually not difficult to strike up a conversation with someone new in a social context. Remember, however, to keep the conversation quite formal initially. If you introduce yourself by your first name, the other person will probably do the same, after which a less formal tone may be adopted.

Don't be surprised if you receive a long-winded answer to the question "How are you?" This phrase is not used as a general greeting as it is in English-speaking countries and will be seen as an opportunity to complain about one's situation, health, or anything else that comes to mind. Likewise, pleasantries such as "Have a nice day" are seen as meaningless and insincere and should be avoided. "Good-bye" ("*do widzenia*") or "see you later" ("*do zobaczenia*") are more than sufficient.

## Shaking Hands, Kissing Hands, Kissing Cheeks

Another potentially awkward moment for foreigners is choosing the appropriate form of "bodily contact," both after being introduced to a Pole and when meeting again after that. These rules are also complex and once again the generation gap is a key factor— younger Poles will be comfortable with modern, Western greetings such as "hello" and a simple handshake.

When meeting someone for the first time or in formal situations, the standard greeting between men is "*dzień dobry*" ("good day" or "hello") followed by a firm, hearty handshake. Between women this is the standard greeting as well, but with a light handshake.

In meetings between a man and a woman, unfortunately, there are no clear rules. Much here depends on the age and relative position of the two people. With younger Poles, "*dzień dobry*" and a handshake are most common. Although the practice is almost extinct, elderly Polish men may bow slightly to kiss a woman's hand as a sign of respect. A respectful handshake is always sufficient for a man being introduced to a Polish woman, regardless of the situation.

In family situations, especially when seeing someone after a long absence or at holiday gatherings, Poles greet each other with a slight embrace and one, two, or three (there is no rule here) kisses on alternate cheeks. If invited to someone's home to meet their family, be prepared for a line to form in front of you with each family member waiting to greet you in this way.

# "A GUEST IN THE HOME IS GOD IN THE HOME"

This old Polish saying is still very much alive. Polish hospitality is exceptional, as is the Polish ability to throw a party. If invited to a Polish home, expect to be well taken care of—it is advisable not to eat beforehand as a meal will probably be prepared in your honor. Even if you are only invited for coffee or tea, it is likely that your host will have bought some fancy cakes. Sample at least a little of what is offered to show appreciation of your host's efforts.

## Meals

Be forewarned if invited for lunch that this will be no small affair. For Poles, a late lunch (*obiad*) tends to be the main meal of the day. Although working hours may make this impossible for many, it still applies on weekends. Expect three or four courses made up of appetizers, soup, and one or two hot dishes, typically with meat. Homemade Polish specialties that should not be missed include dumplings stuffed with meat, cheese, or cabbage and mushroom (*pierogi*), cabbage rolls (*gołąbki*), and pork chops (*schabowy*).

Supper (*kolacja*) is a more modest affair, unless guests are present. Cold appetizers, normally a selection of cheeses, cold meats, pickled herring, and salad, are eaten with bread and normally followed by a small hot dish. The star of the show here, for meat lovers at least, is the assortment of Polish sausages (*kiełbasa*), which can be served hot or cold. *Kolacja*, especially in a large group, is a rather leisurely occasion. People eat at their own pace, while washing the food down with vodka.

## GIVING AND RECEIVING GIFTS

Gift giving is customary in Poland. It is usual to bring something when visiting someone's home, on a first meeting, and on special occasions. Avoid expensive gifts, with the exception of weddings and other very special occasions. They are not expected and may cause embarrassment.

If invited to someone's home, bring your hosts a token gift such as a small souvenir from your country, flowers, chocolates, or a bottle of wine or spirits. Similar gifts are also appropriate for other occasions. In terms of alcohol, a bottle of spirits from your own country will be appreciated, but don't buy vodka. Your host will already have prepared vodka if that's what he or she has in store for the evening.

### Flowers

Polish women may well receive more flowers per capita than anywhere else in the world. Flowers are even given out free on the street on International Women's Day. If taken to someone's home, they should be presented to the lady of the house. Flowers make the perfect gift for a name day or birthday, for both men and women, and florists with impressive selections can be found on practically every street.

Unlike the American custom of buying flowers in bunches of a dozen or half dozen, in Poland flowers for social occasions should always be bought in odd numbers—even numbers are for funerals. The only flowers with special significance are red roses and chrysanthemums. The former, as in Western Europe, signify romance, and the latter are traditionally bought for funerals or when visiting the cemetery.

## DRINKING

Poland, unfortunately, still has a problem with alcoholism. Evidence of this is difficult to miss, in both the cities and the countryside. To help tackle the problem, drinking in public has been made illegal. However, there are no official limits on how many shops in an area can sell alcohol, nor at what times, resulting in alcohol being available for purchase 24/7 in many shops, including gas stations.

Perhaps as a reaction to this, more and more people are turning away from vodka, the traditional Polish spirit, in favor of beer and wine. After a huge rise in the popularity of beer in the quarter century following the end of Communism, industry reports show that beer now accounts for more than half of all alcohol sales in Poland. However, tastes have been changing, and low-alcohol beer, craft and flavored beers, as well as alcohol-free beers and wines, are growing in popularity. The

Friends at a bar in central Warsaw.

sales of imported wine and spirits continue to rise.
Despite this trend, at traditional gatherings it is still
customary to drink vodka.

### Drinking Vodka

In Poland, vodka (*wódka*) is drunk chilled (often
frozen) and neat from shot glasses, with a glass of
juice, mineral water, or cola close by to put out the fire.
It is customary to drink in a series of toasts and not to
sip at your own pace. Normally the host or most senior
person proposes the toasts, but as the evening moves
on, this duty may be taken up by others. If you find
the pace too brisk, which it usually is for foreigners, it
is better to drink half a shot at a time than to miss out
on a round. It is the responsibility of the host, or the

Żubrówka, vodka flavored with bison grass (*Hierochloe odorata*).

person about to propose a toast, to fill the glasses of
the others. Do not fill your own glass without doing
so for others (there is usually no need to ask) and
always fill your own glass last. Women often pass on
straight vodka in favor of mixed drinks or wine but are
welcome to join in with the men if they so choose.

Drinking vodka is a serious business and, even
among those who enjoy it, is increasingly reserved
for special occasions, celebrations, or parties. For
many, this means every Saturday night. In pubs and
restaurants, however, there is very little difference
between the drinking habits of Poles and those of
Western Europeans. The Polish for "Cheers" is
*Na zdrowie* (pronounced "Naz-droh-vee-ay"), or
"To [your] health."

Recent years have seen a resurgence in the popularity of domestic, flavored vodkas. These are also drunk clean and cold, or may be sipped or taken "down in one" as well as served in cocktails. Flavors include herbal (traditional), mint, honey, black cherry, and, most notably, the aromatic Żubrówka, which often includes a tall blade of grass said to come from the primeval Eastern Białowieża forest where bison roam free.

### Vodka Museum, Warsaw

Despite customs changing with the times and society putting more emphasis on responsible drinking, vodka is still considered part of the Polish national heritage and an essential element of national culture. As such, it deserves its own museum of course! The Vodka Museum is housed in a historical building in Warsaw, and offers guided tours as well as tasting experiences, workshops, and a vodka lounge.

Many Poles also make their own alcohol at home—a typical homemade "*nalewka*" usually has an alcohol content of between 40 and 75 percent and is made by infusing different ingredients in vodka or neutral spirits. Typical ingredients are fruit, berries, herbs, spices, roots, sugar, and honey. *Nalewka* is usually drunk as an aperitif, typically served before and/or after, but not with, a meal in small shot glasses. Herb-infused *nalewka* is meant to be medicinal and is said to help with digestion.

## ROMANCE AND DATING

Not long ago, foreigners living in or visiting Poland were still something of a novelty. The result was that single expats and visitors tended not to stay that way for long. EU membership and budget airlines have brought with them an increase in the number of foreigners both visiting and living in Poland. As a result, Poles having foreign partners is increasingly common. That having been said, cross-cultural dating is often a minefield and Poland is no exception.

Polish men tend to play the role of the old-fashioned gentleman where romance is concerned. This can involve anything from helping a lady with her coat to paying the bill. Women can expect to be greeted with flowers and the evening will often be planned down to the minutest detail. Although traditions are changing, it is generally the man who asks the woman out and plans the date.

Be careful, however, not to mistake a casual trip to the pub with romance in bloom. Poles are perfectly comfortable going out in mixed company on a purely platonic basis.

Although attitudes have changed considerably since the 1990s, the gay scene in most Polish cities is very much underground. Look in local English-language magazines or accompanying websites for

information on gay-friendly venues. Be cautious,
however, as attitudes toward openly gay couples can
be hostile—especially in smaller cities and towns.

## Online Dating

Finding a romantic partner the traditional way can
be a challenge as Poles can seem difficult to approach
with their serious expressions and busy schedules.
It's not appropriate to chat people up in the street
with romantic intentions, and inviting someone you've
only just met on a date is considered suspect. In fact,

simply smiling at strangers can be bewildering for them or seen as eccentric. Online dating therefore is a good and popular alternative way to find a potential partner.

International dating apps such as Tinder and Badoo have approximately 60,000 active users every month and are used for everything from hook-ups and making friends to serious relationships. Their users tend to be younger and more adventurous. It's worth noting that some users may only be looking for a foreigner mainly to practice English with, and your romantic hopes may be dashed!

There are also many large Polish dating apps and websites, the most popular being Sympatia.pl and eDarling.pl. They offer both free and premium membership options. These websites are less casual than international apps such as Tinder and are used mainly by singles over thirty looking for a serious relationship.

# CHAPTER FIVE

# AT HOME

For most Poles, home is not just your residence but a social meeting place where the door is always open to friends and family.

## THE POLISH FAMILY

The family is central to Polish culture. Different generations of the same family keep in regular contact and a great many Poles make a weekly migration to their family home for the weekend.

### Children

The statistically average Polish family has 1.4 children (down from 2 in 1990), a rate very similar to that of Western European countries, despite the strong objection of the Catholic Church to contraception. This rate is continuing to fall as the demands of the free-market economy leave people with less time to spend with their families.

Foreigners may find the degree to which parents and grandparents pamper their children excessive. It is unheard of to take a child out in any season but summer without first bundling the little one up in layers of clothing, hats, mittens, and the like. Foreigners who fail to do the same with their own children will meet with the disapproving gaze and comments of nearly every *babcia* (grandmother) they come across. A similar attitude prevails when it comes to finding day care or a school for a child. Great care is taken that the school meets the parents' rigorous standards, and distance has little bearing on this decision.

This very protective attitude usually lasts till the child is a young teenager, after which parents give their

Family outing to Morskie Oko ("Eye of the Sea") lake in the Tatry Mountains.

children much greater freedom. It is usual, for example, for groups of teenagers to take vacations together without any adult supervision.

Young people have the status of minors until their eighteenth birthday, after which they enjoy such freedoms as the right to vote, and, more clearly evident, the right to drink legally. Many pubs and clubs, especially in the cities, are full of eighteen- to twenty-year-olds.

## Senior Citizens

It is quite common for retired people to live with their married children and help in the house and with the grandchildren. Such a situation serves a dual purpose since many senior citizens accept financial help from their children as the government pension of approximately US $540 a month is not enough to support an independent life. On the other hand, grandparents are often heavily involved in childcare, taking the place of nannies for busy working parents. Some public preschools are open until 3:00 p.m. only, while most people leave work at 5:00 or 6:00 p.m., making grandparental assistance invaluable. Nursing homes are still not very common and too expensive for most families. People without family members to help them out financially or with accommodation find it very difficult to make ends meet.

The elderly are respected in Polish society. People will often give up their place in a line or their seat in a bus, tram, or train to an elderly person.

## THE POLISH HOME

There is great variation in the available housing stock. The apartment market is more or less evenly split between old Communist-era blocks and newly developed housing estates. Since social housing is limited, poorly maintained, and difficult to get into, many Poles dream of owning their home. However, building a house in the suburbs remains an aspiration due to the unaffordable cost and high mortgage rates.

A generation ago, parents would build their houses with a "bigger the better" attitude, hoping one day to share them with their children and grandchildren. As many young people migrate to the cities, however, more and more of these houses have been abandoned or only have one or two occupants. Meanwhile, the price per square meter in the cities has skyrocketed, making it increasingly difficult for most young people to buy their own home. Property developers have come up with novel ways of cashing in on the unaffordability of city-center apartments. One innovation is the "micro apartment," which often has no balcony, no windows, and sometimes a shared kitchen and bathroom. More of a dormitory than a home, it is being offered as an option for first-time buyers. While individuals struggle to get a foot on the property ladder, investors are buying up apartments to profit on the high rental, making the market increasingly competitive. Other developers turn their apartments into short-term rentals such as on Airbnb, a market that is still largely unregulated in Poland.

## RENTING AN APARTMENT

Apartments are typically rented directly from the individual owner. The best way to go about this, especially for a foreigner, is through a real-estate agency. Ask a friend if they can recommend a good one, but even if you don't have a recommendation you'll find estate agents to be generally honest and trustworthy. The standard agent's fee is a one-off payment of 50 percent of one month's rent. An alternative to agents is to look for online ads with the help of a Polish speaker. However, many of the telephone numbers in the ads turn out to be the numbers of estate agents and not the individual owners.

An unfurnished apartment typically comes with electrical fixtures and basic kitchen and bathroom cupboards. An apartment listed as furnished could mean anything from fully furnished to a bed, table, and chair. Be forewarned that many apartments for rent will be furnished with very old, worn-out items.

## APPLIANCES

Smaller apartments are usually fitted with a small washing machine in a corner of the kitchen or bathroom. Tumble dryers are something of a luxury, and are normally found only in larger houses. Dishwashers are not as common in apartments as in houses. Outlets in Poland are the standard two-prong, 220-volt European standard, and adapters for small American appliances are readily available in hardware or electronics shops.

When not working, the Poles tend to watch a lot of television by European standards, although less than Americans. Among older generations, it is not unusual for the television to be left on even when someone is entertaining. Guests may find themselves seated around the table, enjoying a meal, while watching the news, a film, or a sporting event. It is becoming less common for young people to own a TV, however. If they do, it is more likely to be used as a screen for a games console or as a streaming platform than to watch terrestrial television channels. Laptops and smartphones have been slowly overtaking television as the main source of entertainment.

## EVERYDAY SHOPPING

Supermarkets exist in abundance and have become part of everyday life. Many people buy their non-perishable goods at Western-style supermarkets while preferring to buy fresh produce at the market. American-style shopping malls are common in the larger cities and are extremely popular, especially during the long Polish winter when strolling down the main street isn't so pleasant. Teenagers often hang out at shopping mall food courts after school, as they are seen as a safe and cheap place to meet.

Corner shops are everywhere, even in the smallest village, and often carry everything from fresh produce and meat to a range of spirits. Such shops used to be at the heart of the local community and were places for locals to meet and gossip. In recent years, however,

Fresh fruit and vegetable market in the district of Kazimierz, Kraków.

chain stores and small supermarket outlets have been taking over, with many small corner shops no longer able to compete. Recently there has been a huge growth of discount supermarkets offering cheaper products and own brands, which have overtaken many large supermarket chains in popularity.

## ONLINE SHOPPING

The Covid-19 pandemic added to the already impressive growth in online shopping in Poland. Practically every kind of shop, from supermarket chains to small specialty boutiques, now have an online presence. Allegro is Poland's eBay equivalent, and Amazon has recently set up shop in the country. Foodies can now even have boxes of fresh fruit and vegetables delivered to their homes on a subscription basis. Several companies now offer app-based deliveries, which have become very popular throughout the country (see Useful Apps, page 198, for more).

## WORK

Most middle-aged Poles, who went through the transition from state socialism to a free-market economy, have experienced huge changes in their lives. To begin with, under the socialist system there was full employment, which resulted in overemployment, that is, too many people to do too little work. This situation, coupled with the increasingly negative attitude toward the state in the 1980s, resulted in an abysmal work ethic. The upside of this state of affairs was that working days were short, typically 8:00 a.m. to 3:00 p.m., and families spent a great deal of time together.

The contrast between then and now is extreme. Despite the high profile of trade unions in Poland, most workers have very few rights, and office workers in particular are often expected to work ten-hour days with no additional overtime payment. With a minimum wage of approximately US $5.50 per hour, many people hold down two jobs in order to get by.

## EDUCATION

On the face of it, the education system in Poland is a success. The country has one of the world's highest adult literacy rates, at 99 percent. In recent years, however, there has been much discussion in the press regarding the level of literacy among adults, especially those living in small villages in the countryside. It has been estimated that about one-third of adults have difficulty understanding what is written in a standard daily newspaper.

Sweeping reforms to the state education system introduced in the 1998–99 school year targeted deficiencies in the old system, largely unchanged since Communist times. The reforms, however, did not address the key problem of teachers' pay. With salaries often lower than US $1,000 per month, many competent teachers have left the profession and young people are reluctant to consider education as a career.

Under the current system, preschool education (*zerówka*) is compulsory from the age of six. From seven to fifteen children attend primary school for eight years, after which they enter secondary school. Secondary school lasts for four years, and pupils can choose between an academic school preparing them for university entry (a *liceum*), or a technical school that prepares them for employment as a skilled worker (a *technikum* or *zawodówka*). Students normally graduate from academic secondary schools at nineteen years of age and sit the national "Matura" final exams. The results of these exams are crucial in securing a place at a good university.

University enrolment has been very high over the past twenty years, as has the number of students going on to postgraduate studies. The current economic

Atrium of the main building of Warsaw University of Technology.

climate provides few opportunities for those without a
university education. There is, however, a growing need
for blue-collar workers such as plumbers, electricians,
truck drivers, and builders, as many skilled Polish
workers have moved to higher-wage countries.

## THE CITY AND THE COUNTRYSIDE

Once again, the difference between the lifestyles of
those living in large cities and those in the countryside
must be stressed. City dwellers tend to work longer
hours, have a superior financial position, and lead
much less traditional lives than their rural compatriots.

The fast pace of Warsaw, especially, is a far cry from life in the country.

One needs only to travel twenty miles from the city to see the contrast. In the countryside it is common to see villagers, elderly women in particular, sitting on benches outside their homes, on the street, watching the world go by. Elderly men still tip their hats when they wish "*dzień dobry*" ("Good day") to passersby and spend hours outside the village shop chatting with other locals.

### Country Ways

Two foreigners were walking through a small village on a sunny day when the heavens opened and they took refuge under the eaves of an old barn next to a run-down farmhouse. After some minutes the front door opened and a man motioned for them to come in. Surprised that his guests didn't speak Polish, the farmer summoned his daughter to translate. He welcomed them to his home and prepared a table of bread, butter, cheese, and ham. The customary bottle of vodka appeared and for the next three hours the group ate, drank, and exchanged stories. When it was time to move on, the daughter produced a bag full of homemade cheeses and ham for the departing guests.

# CHAPTER SIX

# TIME OUT

Among the positive changes that have come about since the end of Communism has been the exponential growth in the number of possible ways of spending one's free time. Cinemas, theaters, pubs, clubs, restaurants, shopping malls, and recreation centers are all available today. Despite this profusion of alternatives, however, the traditional Polish passion for the great outdoors is undiminished.

During long weekends and holidays the cities empty and their inhabitants head *en masse* for the seaside, lakes, mountains, or family homes in the countryside. Although the Poles work long hours, they have generous vacation breaks, and few would even contemplate spending their free days at home. Foreign vacations have also become extremely popular as the price of trips to destinations such as Southern Europe, North Africa, and the Alps has dropped.

A "milk bar" in Gdańsk. These are cheap and cheerful cafeterias serving wholesome food.

## EATING OUT

It wasn't long ago that even in large cities there were only two possibilities available to diners. There were cheap bars offering little more than greasy cutlets, boiled potatoes, and sauerkraut. In fact, in the 1980s even that would have been a lucky find. At the other extreme were posh, very expensive restaurants, although the food and service rarely lived up to the prices. Today, however, thanks largely to greatly increased competition, a wealth of possibilities exists for those in search of a satisfying dining experience at a very reasonable price.

It is not common for restaurants to display their menus outside or in the window, but it is perfectly acceptable to enter and ask to see the *karta* (menu).

In restaurants and cafés one can generally find an English translation of the menu, though this can often be as difficult to understand as the Polish version! Milk bars, cheap, self-service cafeterias that were common in the Communist era, are coming back into fashion, but you'll be hard-pressed to find an English menu in them or an employee who can translate.

Vegetarianism, veganism, and "flexitarianism" are becoming increasingly popular. Plant-based dishes have gone from being near impossible to find to being a staple of the menu in most restaurants. Most large Polish towns and cities now have dedicated vegetarian or vegan restaurants, and Warsaw was recently listed as one of the world's top vegan-friendly cities!

Smoking and vaping are forbidden in restaurants, bars, and clubs in Poland.

### Ethnic Cuisine

The range of ethnic restaurants used to be very limited, but in recent years the Poles have become much more adventurous from a culinary perspective. Italian, Chinese, Turkish, and Greek cuisines are well represented and other ethnic restaurants are constantly popping up. North African and Balkan cafés and restaurants are well worth seeking out. In summer there are weekend "breakfast markets" and food-truck festivals where you can sample a wide range of international cuisines. In Warsaw city center, near the Ochota train station, there is a permanent street-food market called "Nocny market," where you can find anything from tacos to takoyaki.

Clockwise from top left: *pierogi* dumplings served with fried bacon, sour cream, and dill; *placki*, shallow-fried potato pancakes; *barszcz*, beetroot soup, with small mushroom-filled dumplings; and *gołąbki* cabbage rolls with a minced beef and rice stuffing.

## Polish Cuisine

As for Polish cuisine, it is not as easy as one would think to sample local specialities prepared to the same standard as foreign dishes. Traditional Polish food is regarded (and rightfully so) as being best prepared at home. Try a Polish dish in a restaurant and it is very likely that your Polish colleague will comment that their mother or grandmother prepares it in a different and superior way. That having been said, traditional Polish cuisine and restaurants have seen a resurgence in popularity. Ask a Polish acquaintance to recommend a place and, if possible, to join you to help you work through the menu.

Polish specialities well worth trying include *żurek* (a creamy, sour soup with sausage and boiled egg), *gołąbki* (stuffed cabbage rolls), *placki* (potato pancakes), *bigos* (traditional stew), and *pierogi* (dumplings, usually stuffed with meat, cabbage, or white cheese).

## Coffee and Tea

If vodka is Poland's national drink, then tea must be the second. Tea is drunk in huge quantities by both young and old, and it is normally taken with a slice of lemon and no milk. In fact, you may receive strange looks when asking for milk with your tea as it is normally only pregnant and breast-feeding women who drink it this way.

Coffee has become increasingly popular, although some of the serving methods may cause aficionados to cringe. For years, when coffee was hard to come by and coffeemakers were virtually unheard of, Poles made what was erroneously referred to as "Turkish coffee" (*kawa po Turecku*). This involves putting a spoonful or two of regular ground coffee into a cup, then adding boiling water and stirring. Fortunately, the only place you may inadvertently be served "Turkish coffee" these days is in one of the cheapest bars. Beware when taking that last sip or you may end up with coffee grounds in your teeth. At home, however, many older Poles still prepare their coffee this way, although instant is also popular. Most cafés and restaurants today serve coffee from espresso machines. Specialty coffee shops are becoming popular with many young Poles who eschew

Starbucks and other large chains in favor of smaller, independently owned alternatives.

## Drinks

As we have seen, vodka is widely drunk at home on special occasions, or at parties. In restaurants, pubs, and cafés it is generally only drunk by groups of people (usually men) celebrating. It is not a casual drink and so is less popular than beer and wine when Poles go out. Beer, in fact, has become very popular in recent years with both men and women, of all ages and social classes. It is certainly the drink of choice for young Poles.

Polish beers are very good. Lagers are most common, with leading brands named after regions or towns such as Żywiec, Tyskie, and Okocim. Craft beers, flavored beers, porter, and non-alcoholic beers have become popular alternatives.

Bar goers during a night out in Warsaw.

Although Poland is not a wine-producing country, wine, too, is growing in popularity. Reasonably priced quality wines from the Balkans can be found in most shops and restaurants.

---

### WHERE TO DRINK

The Polish word "bar" does not mean a place to drink, but rather a cheap, simple place to get a bite to eat—something between a cafeteria and a café. It may or may not be licensed to serve alcohol.

While pub culture may not exist in Poland in the British sense, pubs have become increasingly popular and tend to be lively spots with a good atmosphere. To wet your whistle, it is best to find a pub or café where the atmosphere is usually cosy and quiet. Cafés close relatively early, whereas pubs generally close at 11:00 p.m., but may well remain open till sunrise.

---

## Service

Despite horror stories from the 1980s and early '90s about the standards of service in Poland (many of them true), today's reality is greatly different. In large cities, with the exception of cheap bars or "drink bars," standards are very similar to most Western

European countries. However, you may just occasionally experience the rudeness and reluctance of Communist-era service. This can happen in restaurants of every type.

### *TIPPING*

Rules regarding tipping are not written in stone, and many diners do not leave anything. Because of this, perhaps, tips are very much appreciated by the staff. Generally speaking, if the service is satisfactory a tip of 10 to 20 percent is appropriate.

Be careful not to say "thank you" when paying your bill unless you intend to leave the change as a tip. "Thank you" (*"dziękuję"*) is a euphemism for "keep the change" when paying a bill. This is why your thanks when paying a bill will always be greeted with a broad smile.

## NIGHTLIFE

The nighttime scene varies greatly from city to city, with virtually nothing happening in smaller towns. The Old Town Square in Kraków is abuzz with pub hoppers till the wee hours, while in the industrial city of Katowice it can be a challenge to find anything open after 10:00 p.m. Generally speaking, however, Polish pubs have no strict regulations regarding last calls, and many advertise themselves as staying open "till the last guest." It's usually not difficult to find a place open till 1:00 or 2:00 a.m. in Warsaw or Kraków.

As for nightclubs and discos, there's no point showing up before 11:00 p.m. as nothing much will be happening. The action starts between 11:00 p.m. and midnight and usually lasts till around 3:00 a.m. Practically all nightclubs charge an entrance fee, usually 20 or 30 złoty. Many clubs also have strict dress codes, enforced by intimidating-looking bouncers, so it's best to check on the club's website before turning up. Poles, young and old, love to dance, so put on your dancing shoes!

## TOURIST SHOPPING

Shopping in Poland's large cities differs little from elsewhere in Europe. You can find high-quality, expensive boutiques and specialty shops in the center or Old Town intermixed with cafés, delicatessens, and souvenir shops.

Polish markets are worth experiencing, whether they're flower markets, farmers' markets, or those found in larger cities with traders selling anything under the sun. If possible, ask a Polish friend or colleague to recommend a good market and to accompany you as it will be difficult to cope without a translator. It is worth noting that market traders rarely haggle and the price you see is probably what you'll have to pay, although no offense will be taken if you try.

Hand-painted souvenir ceramic plates.

Shopping hours in Poland are quite generous by European standards. Main street stores are typically open from 8:00 a.m. till 9:00 p.m., Mondays to Fridays, and from 9:00 a.m. to 3:00 p.m. on Saturdays. Shopping centers and supermarkets are usually open from 9:00 a.m. till 10:00 p.m., Monday through Saturday, and varying hours on Sundays.

Although a law banning trade on Sundays has been introduced, many convenience stores are open on Sundays from 10:00 a.m to 6:00 p.m. There are some exceptions to the Sunday trading law, including art galleries and waiting rooms, so in a typical Polish *"kombinowanie"* way of thinking, some stores have cheekily put up a painting and called themselves art galleries, or a plastic chair in order to be considered a waiting room, as a way to stay open throughout the weekend.

## Souvenirs

Among the most sought-after purchases for foreigners in Poland are amber, silver, crystal, vodka, pottery, and handmade craft items. Lace tablecloths and pottery from Bolesławiec in the south of Poland are also very popular. Some Polish brands of cosmetics and skincare products are well known around the world, so it's worth grabbing some items from Ziaja or Inglot. Although these products may be cheaper in Poland than in most other European countries, be aware that prices in tourist areas such as Old Town squares and hotel gift shops may be considerably higher than elsewhere in the country.

## MONEY

Although Poland is a member of the European Union, it does not use the single EU currency. The Polish złoty (PLN) is the country's currency and one złoty is made up of 100 groszy. Banknotes are in denominations of 10, 20, 50, 100, 200, and 500 złoty.

All major Western currencies are easily exchanged in any city at banks, hotels, or exchange kiosks, called *kantor* in Polish. It is worth changing your money in a *kantor* as they are perfectly safe and trustworthy, with better exchange rates than banks and hotels. Different *kantors* will have slightly different rates, so it may be worth comparing a few if changing a large sum. The rate displayed outside the *kantor* is the actual rate with no additional fees or charges. If you are exchanging large sums, it may be worth comparing exchange rates online. Better rates than advertised can often be negotiated for large amounts (US $500 or more for example).

Traveler's checks should be cashed at your hotel or in a bank, as they are not normally accepted in shops. Visa and Eurocard/Mastercard are accepted in most shops and restaurants, as are bank cards compatible with the Euronet network. Bank machines are easy to find and are commonly located in shopping centers, gas stations, supermarkets, shopping streets, and tourist areas, as well as in any bank.

Since personal checks are not used in Poland, personal or large financial transactions are normally settled by bank transfer. A Polish bank account, therefore, may prove useful for anyone staying for an extended period of time. Bank accounts are easy to open for foreigners and require only standard documents.

## MUSEUMS

Poland hosts a number of impressive museums and galleries, mostly in the larger towns and cities. Most charge a modest admission fee, and the visitors tend to be a combination of well-educated Poles, foreign tourists, and children on school trips. If possible, take time to visit the National Museum, Wilanów Palace, and the POLIN Museum of the History of Polish Jews in Warsaw; the Jagiellonian University Museum, the Wawel

The neoclassical Łazienki Palace Museum in the grounds of Warsaw's Royal Baths Park.

The iconic leaning tower and glass façade of the Museum of the Second World War, Gdańsk.

The medieval Niedzica Castle on the shores of Czorsztyn Lake is now a historical museum.

Royal Castle Museum, and MOCAK: the Museum of Contemporary Art in Kraków; and the Museum of the Second World War in Gdańsk.

## THE PERFORMING ARTS

### Polish Theater

Theater as an institution has played a special role in Polish culture. Throughout the period of political censorship under the Communist regime many playwrights managed to outsmart the censors and slip derogatory references to the system into their plays. Today the theater remains popular with young and old alike, whether it's traditional, experimental, or modern. Several theater companies have won international acclaim, and all Polish cities have a number of theaters to

Kraków's nineteenth-century eclectic-style Juliusz Słowacki Theater.

choose from. A must for lovers of experimental theater is the Witkiewicz Theater in the historic mountain resort town of Zakopane. It is well worth the trip, despite the fact that the repertoire is entirely in Polish.

A particular form of theater that epitomizes the paradoxical nature of Polish culture is cabaret, which in Poland lies somewhere between the familiar song-and-dance routines of the West and satire. Cabaret can be found in any size of venue, from small restaurants to the largest theaters, and is a favorite on television. No politician or celebrity is safe from the performers' barbs. More often parodied than any individual, however, is Poland itself, or perhaps more accurately, Polishness. Typically, the various cabaret acts manage to walk a fine line of showing pride in the country while making fun of it at the same time.

## Opera and Ballet

In the years of Communism, factory workers and miners were taken for nights out to the opera or ballet as part of the attempt to make high culture available to the masses. Although the experiment had limited success, one positive element remains—the price of tickets. Polish opera and ballet companies are of a high standard and are still subsidized, with ticket prices that actually do make high culture accessible to all. Most companies feature international and Polish composers in their repertoires. Many cities have their own ballet and opera houses, but Warsaw's Grand Theater (Teatr Wielki), one of the largest theaters in Europe, is home to opera, classical music, and ballet performances.

## Polski Hip-Hop

The most popular music in the country tends to be that of the same Western artists heard around the world; however, there are a number of very popular home-grown Polish musicians, including Polish rappers. Starting from humble beginnings in the mid-1990s, the Polish hip-hop scene has grown into a major industry with a huge following, and though it was once enjoyed by urban youngsters alone, today the genre has fans across the country.

## Cinema

Going to the movies is very popular in the cities, especially among the young. There is no shortage of cinemas, including modern multiplex facilities, often located in shopping centers. The good news for visitors in the mood for a film is that foreign-language films are screened with their original soundtracks with Polish subtitles. Smaller towns rarely have facilities to match those in the cities.

Poland is known internationally for its acclaimed directors. Among these are Roman Polański, Andrzej Wajda, and the late Krzysztof Kieślowski.

## OUTDOOR ACTIVITIES

The Poles have a great love for the outdoors, and while this may not be evident on a winter's day in Warsaw, take a trip to one of the country's many national or regional parks on a sunny day to see for yourself. Poland has much to offer both summer and winter sports enthusiasts.

### Walking and Hiking

Walking and hiking are favorite pastimes. Trails are well-marked, and there are clear, concise tourist site maps. Destinations for walking and hiking vacations are the national parks and various historical sites. The Białowieża National Park to the east of the country on the Belarusian border has the largest original lowland forest in Europe and is a paradise for those who love walking in the woods.

The Tatry, Sudety, Pieniny, and Bieszczady Mountains, all in the south of the country, offer excellent hiking with a well-developed tourist infrastructure, including a wide range of

The all-seasons cable car from Kuźnice to the top of Kasprowy Wierch in the western Tatry range.

accommodation to choose from. It's customary to wish "good day" ("*dzień dobry*") or "hi" ("*cześć*") to any fellow hikers you pass in the mountains.

In Polish cities most parks, especially at the weekends, are full of cyclists, joggers, Nordic walkers, and even yoga classes.

## Cycling

Recreational cycling has become very popular in recent years and the network of cycling paths is constantly being expanded and modernized. In big cities, you can usually find a cycle path to take you where you need to go, and, if not, it's fine to cycle in the street. Avoid cycling on sidewalks as this is illegal and fines are not uncommon. In the countryside, bicycles are still used more as a practical means of transportation than a form of recreation.

App-based bike rentals are popular in cities throughout the country. It's also easy to find cycling groups of different levels on social media sites, and anyone can join them on trips free of charge.

Be extremely careful to lock your bike any time it is left unattended, however. Bicycle theft is big business in Poland.

## Skiing

All the mountain ranges in the south of the country offer alpine skiing facilities. The Tatry Mountains, being the highest, generally have the best conditions and the most reliable snow. The quality of lifts and snow grooming equipment can be disappointing, however, for those used to skiing in Western European resorts, as can the long lines for the lifts.

## Sailing

The Mazury Lakes, sixty miles northeast of Warsaw, is the place to go for sailing. On a hot summer's day the lakes and lakeshore beer gardens come alive with sailing enthusiasts. It is possible to rent a boat with or without a crew.

The Baltic Sea also provides opportunities for sailing, but the winds, waves, and unpredictable weather make it less popular than the lakes for weekend sailors.

# CHAPTER SEVEN

# TRAVEL, HEALTH, & SAFETY

Getting from A to B in Poland can be a trying experience, depending on your destination. The good news is that traveling between major cities is quick, reliable, and inexpensive. The bad news is that if your destination is a little off the beaten path there may be no good news, except for an interesting cultural experience.  Transportation links are constantly improving, however, as more money flows into the infrastructure.

## ENTERING POLAND

If flying to Poland, you will most likely arrive in either Warsaw or Kraków, although international flights are also available to Bydogoszcz, Katowice, Poznań, Szczecin, and Wrocław. Warsaw now has a second international airport, so make sure to check which one your flight arrives at or departs from. The new airport (Warsaw Modlin) is used by budget airlines flying to and from other European destinations. The main airlines continue to use Warsaw Chopin Airport, which is much closer to the city center and has better facilities than its new competitor. There are many direct intercity rail links to Berlin, Prague, Budapest, and Vienna.

## Visas

With Poland's entry to the European Union, the entry requirements have undergone many changes and these changes are continuing. Please verify any of the information given below with your local Polish consulate. For visits of up to ninety days' duration, no visa is required for citizens of the USA and EU member states, including other new accession states.

## Passport Control and Customs

Generally speaking, this is a straightforward matter, no different from that in Western EU member states. Currency declarations are a thing of the past, as are intrusive customs inspections. European travelers from countries of the Schengen Area (the EU's border-free area) will have an easier time of it than those from non-Schengen countries or outside the EU, who may be held up at passport control.

## GETTING AROUND

### By Rail

There are five standards of train (*pociąg*) in Poland: Express InterCity Premium, InterCity/EuroCity, express (*ekspresowy*), fast train (*pośpieszny*), and commuter train (*osobowy*).

Express InterCity Premium connections are limited and are the most expensive option, but they are quick and comfortable. These Pendolino trains can reach a speed of just over 180 mph (290 kmph) and travel from Warsaw to Kraków in two hours and twenty minutes. The tickets are only slightly more expensive than the next quickest option, so it's worth considering. Buying your tickets early can result in significant savings.

InterCity and EuroCity trains travel between major cities, usually nonstop, with the latter servicing certain international routes. As well as being a fast, efficient means of transportation, these trains are very comfortable and have complimentary tea or coffee and a restaurant car. Reservations are required for both first and second class.

Express trains cover more routes than the InterCity service and are equally fast, but with older carriages, no complimentary tea and coffee, and a self-service bar car. Reservations are compulsory for both classes on express trains.

Fast trains travel similar routes to the InterCity and Express services but with many more stops. The standard of the carriages may be considerably lower and there may or may not be a bar car. Reservations on fast trains are optional, but recommended, especially on busy routes at peak hours.

Commuter trains used to have a bad reputation as slow, overcrowded, and in poor condition. However, most of the old trains have been replaced with new carriages equipped with air conditioning, well-kept toilets, charging points for phones and laptops, and sometimes even free Wi-Fi. Nevertheless, trains servicing the more remote areas may still be the older stock. Their average speed is about 20 mph (32 kmph) and they stop at just about every village on the way, even if it consists of three houses, eight people, and twelve cows. If you must reach a small town or village and are without a car this, unfortunately, may be your only option.

Tickets for all trains can be purchased at the station, either at the counter or from a machine, at a travel agent, or on board with a small surcharge. Different train operators sometimes offer services on the same lines, so make sure to buy the appropriate ticket for each service. Be careful with your bags on trains, especially when traveling at night and on international routes.

It is common for passengers entering a long-distance train compartment to wish "Good day" ("*dzień dobry*") to each other upon entering and "Good-bye" ("*do widzenia*") when leaving. In case you haven't got a reserved seat, it's polite to ask if a seat is free (*wolne*) before claiming it. It is usually possible to take a bicycle or dog with you, but do check for extra fees when purchasing your ticket.

## By Car

For reaching locations other than city centers, driving is the most convenient option. It would be a big advantage, however, if you could get a Polish colleague to drive

The Rędziński Bridge carrying traffic over the Odra River in Wrocław.

you, as Polish roads and motorists can make driving a challenge. Despite massive investment in the highway network, the state of the roads is one of the most visible signs that Poland still lags behind the EU's Western member states in economic development. Polish drivers can be very aggressive and will think nothing of cruising along at 60 mph (97 kmph) or more on a narrow road, swerving to avoid the potholes that make many roads an obstacle course.

To drive in Poland, holders of a European driver's license do not require any other documents. In addition to a valid driver's license, anyone without a European license will need to obtain an international driver's permit from their automobile association before leaving for Poland.

Road signs and markings are of the standard European type, so non-European drivers should consult a driver's guide to make sense of it all. Finally, beware of tram lines in cities. Trams have the right of way in all situations, and wet or icy tracks are a hazard.

In most town and city centers, on-street parking must be paid for on weekdays between 8:00 a.m and 8:00 p.m. Simply find the nearest parking machine, pay for the chosen length of time, and display the ticket in your car. Payment is by cash, card, or app. On national holidays and weekends on-street parking is free in most places.

## By Bus

Traveling by bus in Poland can be anything from a quick, comfortable, air-conditioned ride to an endurance test involving standing in an overcrowded coach bouncing over bumpy roads and either sweltering in the heat or freezing to death, depending on the season. It's unlikely you'll end up doing the latter by mistake, but by purchasing your ticket through a travel agent you should safely avoid a shocking cultural experience.

On the other hand, traveling to Poland from Western Europe by bus is predictably comfortable, as only newer, high-standard vehicles are used on these routes. The bus is usually only marginally slower than the train and can be considerably cheaper. Unsurprisingly, it tends to be the transportation of

choice for Polish students on vacation. A one-way
bus ride between Warsaw and Kraków usually takes
about four and a half hours and can cost as little as
50 złoty (US $11).

## By Plane

Flying between Polish cities has become much cheaper
in recent years, especially at weekend rates. The only
problem is that for many routes, Warsaw to Kraków
for example, by the time you get to the airport, wait to
board, and take a taxi after arriving at your destination,
you could have saved money by taking the train. From
the center of Warsaw to the center of Kraków takes
two and a half hours by express or InterCity train.
This would be hard to beat by plane as at least one
hour would probably be spent getting to and from
the airports. A local travel agent can help you plan
the best way of getting to where you want to go.

## LOCAL TRANSPORTATION

### Public Transportation

The standard of public transportation varies greatly
depending on where in the country you are. In larger
cities the service is quite efficient and very affordable.
Virtually all major cities have two main forms of public
transportation: tram and bus. The old Communist-
era trams and buses have, for the most part, been
replaced by modern, air-conditioned ones. Trams are
a better bet if you are in a rush as they avoid most of

Metro entrance by night, Warsaw.

the traffic jams. Both trams and buses run regularly
from approximately 4:00 a.m. to midnight, Monday
to Saturday, with a reduced service on Sundays and
public holidays. In large cities on weekdays you
shouldn't have to wait for a tram or bus for more than
ten or fifteen minutes. Warsaw has the country's only
subway service (*metro*), which consists of a north–
south line and an east–west line.

Each city issues its own transit tickets, which are
valid for all forms of public transportation within the
city. Kiosks, normally located on main streets, and
ticket offices at main stations are the places to buy
a ticket (*bilet*). Failing that, it is usually possible to
purchase a ticket from a machine on the bus or tram.
After boarding the tram or bus your ticket must be

validated in one of the ticket-validating machines. If you're unsure what to do, take your cue from the other passengers. It is also possible to buy single- or multiple-use tickets using apps (moBilet, mPay, SkyCash, zBiletem i jakdojade.pl); however, make sure to read the instructions on ticket validating carefully as some tickets require you to scan a QR code once on board.

If you're going to be in town for a long stint, weekly and monthly tickets are available at the kiosks or at any post office. Tickets are checked randomly by "undercover" ticket inspectors. Fines for traveling without a ticket are the only thing that is not cheap about Polish public transportation, so don't take any chances.

## Taxis

Taxis are a fast, efficient, and cost-effective way of getting around in Polish cities. There is certainly no shortage of taxis in the large cities and you shouldn't have to wait long to find a vacant one. There are, however, a few things to be aware of.

First of all, taxi drivers are generally very honest and will rarely take advantage of foreigners. This is not the case at airports and train stations, however. Never agree to the offer of a ride from a cabbie loitering in the arrivals area asking if you need a taxi, or you will almost certainly be taken for a ride in more ways than one. Go to the taxi information desk in the arrivals area of the airport. The people there will order a proper cab for you with standard rates. This system works very well at Warsaw International Airport.

A plug-in hybrid electric taxi cab in Gdynia.

Not many taxi drivers will speak English, so if your Polish skills are weak or non-existent it's a good idea to write down your destination on a piece of paper, which you can then show to the driver. It is usually possible to request an English-speaking driver if booking a cab online or by phone.

Never take a taxi that does not have a company name and phone number clearly marked on it. If there is simply a rooftop sign bearing the word "Taxi," look for another. Phoning for a taxi is always a good idea. Waiters, waitresses, and office and hotel receptionists will always be happy to call a cab for you.

By law, fares must be displayed in the window. Note, however, that there are higher tariffs at night, on Sundays and holidays, and for trips outside the city limits. Tipping is not very common, but rounding up the fare will always be appreciated.

App-based services such as Uber, Bolt, and FreeNow are also available throughout Poland. These services are generally considered safe, but don't count on your driver speaking English. Many of those apps also offer other means of transportation, such as bikes or scooters, as well as food delivery services.

Car sharing is not widespread in Poland, but there are a number of companies operating in the larger cities, the most popular of which is Traficar. Electric scooter and bike sharing is far more popular and these can be found in towns and cities across the country.

Every Old Town tourist square has horse-drawn carriages. These are predominantly for tourists, apart from the occasional couple on their wedding day.

Horse and carriage in Kraków.

## WHERE TO STAY

Accommodation in Poland comes in all shapes and sizes. Whatever type you choose, the standards of safety and hygiene will generally be high.

While all hotels in Poland use the same five-star rating system as most European countries, this works only as a general guide and can be rather inconsistent. For the sake of comparison, types of accommodation will be covered in three categories: high-end, medium-priced, and budget. Checking online hotel reviews is the best way to find a suitable hotel and avoid an unpleasant surprise.

### High-end Accommodation

Recent years have seen a huge growth in the Polish hotel industry. Supply has increased significantly and as a result prices have dropped while the standards are similar to hotels in Western Europe.

In addition to Western hotel chains, there are many top-class Polish hotels where you can experience a little more local culture. If you have time to visit a resort such as Sopot on the Baltic coast, or Zakopane in the Tatry Mountains, and if your budget allows, a few nights in such a hotel is well worth the investment.

### Medium-priced Accommodation

Much of the drab, Communist-era accommodation that made up this class of hotel has thankfully been replaced by simple but clean and modern chain hotels. In addition, there is a vast choice of smaller, privately owned hotels in this price range. They are often friendlier and cosier than the larger hotels, and are more likely to be located in the old quarters, but they can also be disappointing. Ask a friend or colleague if they can recommend a good hotel or check online reviews.

At the lower end of this price range are pensions (*pensjonat*). Mostly found in smaller towns and tourist resorts, they are often rich in character and located in old buildings. Breakfast is usually included in the price and full board can often be arranged as well.

## Budget Accommodation

Much of the accommodation available in this category is student hostels. Typical student hostels can be found in the large cities, but there are not that many elsewhere in the country. As a result, they tend to be overcrowded and there are often no free places available. Curfews may be strictly enforced, so beware!

Finally, private or shared accommodation can be organized through Internet sites. Providers such as AirBnB, Booking.com, and Couchsurfing are popular and reliable in Poland. As with anywhere else, however, proceed with caution and be sure to check reviews.

## HEALTH

As in other European countries, basic health care and hospitalization are covered by a national health-care system. Non-emergency treatment often involves lengthy waiting times, however, so many Poles (those who can afford it) opt for private health care to deal with routine aches and pains. Apart from waiting times of up to two years, however, the standards of public hospitals and health-care professionals are high.

EU citizens visiting Poland are strongly advised to obtain a European Health Insurance Card (EHIC), which enables holders to access the Polish public health-care system. Non-EU citizens, including those from the UK, are strongly advised to purchase medical insurance before traveling. Private health care providers charge the same rates for Poles and foreign nationals. Their fees are often significantly lower than in other countries, however, making Poland an increasingly attractive health tourism destination. Private dental practices are similarly attractively priced and usually have excellent standards of hygiene, equipment, facilities, and medical staff.

On a final note, there are perhaps proportionately more pharmacies in Poland than anywhere in the world! Look for an *Apteka* (pharmacy) sign, usually associated with a medical cross. All standard medications should be available and names are often similar. Pharmacists often speak enough English to communicate with you and will recommend over-the-counter medication for minor ailments.

## SAFETY

Poland is not a particularly dangerous country, although the change from being an extremely safe country during

Communist times to becoming a country with normal, Western-style dangers has shocked many older Poles.

Overall, this is a pretty safe environment, but there are certain things to beware of. It is advisable to take a taxi at night rather than walk, and to beware of pickpockets in crowded places. While violent crime is rare, petty crime such as pickpocketing is, unfortunately, problematic. This is especially true in the crowded city centers and on public transportation. Keep valuables safely on your person and avoid leaving bags unattended. Also be careful not to leave handbags, wallets, purses, and phones in plain view while sitting outside— especially in outdoor cafés or beer gardens.

Steer clear of groups of football fans, especially before or after matches, and avoid local drunks in drinking establishments who may become interested in you once they hear you speaking a foreign language. Such characters are relatively harmless but can be difficult to get rid of. Make up an excuse, and move on.

In case of any difficulties, call the emergency services on 112, or the police emergency number 997. The police and emergency services are generally reliable and tend to turn up quickly when needed.

# CHAPTER EIGHT

# BUSINESS BRIEFING

Many Western expatriates in Poland have come to the country on business, and until recently a large percentage of the top managers and directors of Western companies operating in Poland were Westerners. This has begun to change, however, and today you are likely to find experienced, qualified Poles in these positions. The fact that so many Polish managers and directors have had substantial contact with Western businesspeople and are familiar with Western business practices gives them an advantage over a foreigner who is unfamiliar with the local business environment. Having at least a basic understanding of how Poles conduct business therefore is crucial for success.

At first glance, Polish business culture seems to be a hodgepodge of old socialist-era networks, hard-selling, fast-talking American sales techniques, and everything in between. While there may be some truth to this impression, there is, in fact, an unwritten code of conduct. Some of these unwritten rules are general and others are specific to particular groups.

## POLISH BUSINESSPEOPLE

In Poland the people you may be doing business with could be young, educated managers, fluent in English and with a very familiar business style. On the other hand, you could find yourself dealing with senior managers whose experience is based upon running elephantine socialist state corporations.

### The Old Guard

Although steadily decreasing in number, some Polish managers today are still former directors of state companies from the 1980s and 1990s. First of all, don't jump to the conclusion that they are old Communist dinosaurs with no idea of how to work in a modern environment. Although there is no shortage of such examples, many managers with experience from the former system are as skilled at making their way in today's reality as they were in yesterday's. Furthermore, they often have contacts in the right places, which is crucial in Polish business.

When meeting such people it is advisable to be more formal than you would be with younger counterparts. Choose a good restaurant if inviting them out, and refrain from addressing them by their first name unless invited to do so.

Such individuals can offer valuable insights into the inner workings of Polish business. They understand the changes and challenges facing the business community and tend to have a wealth of contacts, which can help in a range of situations. This is particularly useful in dealing with the miles of red tape often needed to do business in Poland.

Red tape frustrates Poles and foreigners alike. In fact, the various regulations are often contradictory and seem to change on a daily basis. This is especially true when it comes to tax regulations. Many Poles hoped that integration into the European Union would solve such problems, as Polish regulations had to come into line with those of the EU. The result in many cases, however, has been a duplication of paperwork. To further complicate matters, many Polish regulations are not spelled out clearly, leaving much room for "interpretation" on the part of the government officials who must give their approval. This has led to further opportunities for corruption among civil servants.

## The New Guard

With the large number of graduates with MBAs and other business qualifications from Polish universities, there is a surplus of young, well-educated junior managers. The key for them is experience, and those who have managed to combine their studies with the right professional work experience will have no shortage of opportunities. What they may lack in terms of international experience, they make up for in effort and determination. It is not uncommon for young Polish managers to work more than ten hours per day.

Increasingly, this new breed of manager combines Western education with local knowledge and a fundamental understanding of the preexisting rules of the game inherited from their predecessors. This combination equips them well for the realities of the emerging Polish market and is largely responsible for Poland's impressive, consistent economic growth in the post-Communist period.

## Entrepreneurs

It is hard to find an entrepreneurial spirit elsewhere in Europe to match that of the Poles. The moment state restrictions on private enterprise were eased in 1989, people started to put their savings into small businesses, ranging from produce stalls and hot-dog stands to nationwide franchises. This spirit has survived, buoyed up partly by low wages that force many to find other ways to make ends meet. For the moment, many small shops have weathered the storm of competition from supermarkets and international franchises.

## *Biznesmen*

The term *biznesman,* and the female equivalent *biznesmanka,* is the label applied to a more dubious type of entrepreneur. The stereotypical Polish *biznesman* is involved in some sort of dodgy business, has very poor fashion sense, and will blow most of his fortune on a used, imported (or possibly stolen) BMW or Mercedes. The chances of a foreigner in the country on legitimate business meeting up with such a character are limited, but if you come across someone fitting this description, beware.

## POLISH BUSINESS CULTURE

### Hierarchy

In Communist times state-controlled companies were extremely hierarchical. Not surprisingly, this structure has survived in companies that are still state controlled, as well as those that, although privatized, have retained their senior management.

In this system, senior managers would secure their positions by surrounding themselves with loyal subordinates who restricted access to them by anyone outside the inner circle. Although this type of structure survives intact in relatively few companies, they tend to be very large and the structure very strong. When dealing with the employees of such a company, it is key to ascertain who the decision-makers are and to deal directly with the highest-ranking person you can gain access to. This also applies to any dealings with government departments.

The reality in most companies is markedly different, although certain elements from the old system may survive. Western companies with young Polish managers tend to have a much less hierarchical structure, in which ideas and communication flow freely. Decision-making may, however, still follow a very structured path.

## Personal Contacts

We have already noted that personal networks were crucial in the Communist era and still play an important role in modern Polish society. Nowhere is this more true than in business. Having contacts in the right places can help you to find products, people, and places, ease bureaucratic processes, speed up customs clearances, and generally make business more efficient. When someone tells you they have a friend who can help you, this is, in a sense, an introduction into an informal network.

## Corruption and Bribery

There is no doubt that corruption still exists in Poland, but it does not impinge on everyday life. In 2022 Poland ranked 45th out of 180 countries in Transparency International's Corruption Perceptions Index. In the business sphere, the influx of EU funds has created new opportunities for corrupt practices. For the foreigner doing business there, the best advice is to keep to the moral high ground and not compromise yourself in any ambiguous situations.

Small "gifts" for personal favors are another matter, and much of what would be considered questionable in other countries may simply be normal business practice in Poland. If someone has assisted you with a problem in a way that goes beyond what you would normally have expected of them (that is, they have not been officially paid for this service) and you genuinely appreciate their help, then it is appropriate to give a gift. This could be an invitation to dinner, a bottle of alcohol, or something from your own country, but not cash. Such presents are seen as gifts, whereas cash is seen as a bribe.

### Business Dress

Poland is not Silicon Valley and this is evident in the way businesspeople dress. Very few have the luxury of going to work in casual clothing and formal business dress is the norm. In Polish business, for better or for worse, people are judged by their appearance. Furthermore, dressing well for a meeting shows your counterpart(s) that you value the opportunity to meet them. A smart, stylish suit always makes a good impression. Having said this, many companies have implemented a less prescriptive approach to office attire in recent years.

## FIRST ENCOUNTERS

There is not much about business meetings in Poland that the visitor with a little intercultural experience would find odd or difficult to deal with. Setting up a meeting in the first instance is not always straightforward, however. Polish managers and directors often have PAs, who may also be acting as gatekeepers. Establishing a good rapport with this individual can pay dividends. This can be done by simply showing a genuine interest in their role or asking them questions you may have about Poland. Gifts are not necessary.

### Power Games

When invited to someone's office to meet face to face, it is not at all uncommon to be kept waiting for five to fifteen minutes. The receptionist is likely to tell you that the person you are to meet is with someone else or on the phone. In fact, this is a tactic often used to assert one's authority and to gain power in a relationship.

Another power ploy sometimes used by Poles is to sit at a large, open table in a conference room, even for one-on-one meetings, making the visitor feel awkward and powerless.

### Greetings

When meeting someone for the first time in a business context, you should introduce yourself using both your first and last names and, regardless of gender, shake hands. Later, at a convenient moment, offer your business card. This is normally done sitting down at a table. Make sure that you have a card for everyone present, regardless of their position. Generally the social conventions described in Chapter 4 apply.

### Where Meetings Take Place

Individual or small meetings are likely to take place in the office. For larger group meetings it is common to rent a boardroom in a prestigious hotel, which has the advantage of being a neutral location.

Lunch or dinner meetings in a restaurant are becoming more common, but more as a way of cementing good relations than to hammer out details. Business is discussed but in a rather informal manner and is intermixed with small talk. The person proposing the meeting will generally pay the bill, and it would be seen as awkward to attempt to divide the bill in any way.

If you would like to propose a meeting, ask someone, or indeed your guest, to recommend a good restaurant. Showing an interest in Polish cuisine will always be viewed favorably, as will taking advantage of the opportunity to learn more about Poland. Ask your guest any questions you may have about the country. There is no need to be embarrassed about your ignorance of Polish history or culture—Poles love to enlighten visitors about the situation, both past and present, in their country. Dinner meetings may last well into the night, and if they do it is an indication that things are going well. Breakfast meetings are still virtually unheard of.

## GROUP MEETINGS

Protocol at Polish meetings is usually straightforward. There is not likely to be a formal written agenda. The most senior person present, or the person with whom you've had the most contact, will introduce everybody and lay out the agenda for the day.

Generally speaking, the atmosphere will be relaxed. Poles feel free to speak their minds and often will. Foreigners should do the same or may be seen as weak or lacking ideas. If you have facts and figures to back up your points, ideas, or proposals, make sure you have them to hand in a presentable format. Meetings in Poland are often called to present and discuss facts and findings, rather than to brainstorm new ideas.

### Punctuality

It is vital to be well turned out and punctual for your first meeting. Subsequently, although it's never a bad thing to be on time, don't panic if you arrive ten minutes late for a business meeting. Punctuality is not a quality on which people are judged in Poland, although repeatedly showing up late may be seen as a reflection of your level of respect for the other party.

## PRESENTATIONS

Most Polish offices are well equipped with all the hardware you need for a presentation. Multimedia (PowerPoint style) presentations are becoming the norm in many companies. It always makes a good impression on Poles if you accompany your presentation with data and facts, although it may not be expected. Try to make eye contact with everyone in the room, not just the most senior person. It is fine to start with a light anecdote, only be careful with jokes as cultural differences may mean that your Polish audience won't find them as funny as your colleagues back home. It is best to get down to business fairly soon after starting. Finally, don't feel offended if you are interrupted—questions show interest, and will be asked when they arise rather than kept till the end of the presentation.

### Don't Panic

An American businesswoman was taking part in a meeting held in a conference room at the Marriott Hotel in Warsaw. After problems with transportation, she arrived ten minutes late and entered the room out of breath, apologizing profusely. Those Polish participants who had already arrived (fewer than half) found it entertaining that anyone would panic over a mere ten minutes. They explained that the first fifteen minutes or so were used for mingling and small talk, only after which would business begin.

## NEGOTIATIONS

There is no negotiating style that can be said to be specifically Polish. As with other aspects of business in Poland, much depends on the age and amount of international experience of the person with whom you are dealing. Once again, clear communication is the key. If your Polish counterpart has the impression that you are behaving in a condescending manner, or that you don't view them as equal in your negotiations, they may react in a way that can best be described as inflexible and potentially counterproductive.

On the whole, as long as you are clear and open in your negotiations, you can expect the same from the other side. As good personal relations are important in business, a successful conclusion to your talks can be the first step in a strong and lasting partnership.

### Closing Deals

It is always a good idea to follow up a meeting by putting all agreements down on paper or in an e-mail, even if there is no formal document to be signed. This can simply be a letter of understanding that outlines the conclusions reached during negotiations as well as the obligations each party is to undertake.

## CONTRACTS

Polish civil law is based on the continental legal system. Contracts in business are respected and treated much as they would be in most Western countries. The Polish Language Act requires the use of the Polish language in contracts when at least one party is a Polish entity. Agreements in other languages may exist, but under the Act the Polish-language version is considered binding.

The standard procedure is that following negotiations one of the sides (usually the host) will have their lawyers draw up a draft contract. This will be sent to you and any objections or proposed changes will be taken seriously and another meeting called to discuss them if necessary. It is not common to come to such meetings with a team of lawyers, contract in hand, and to pressurize for a signature.

Disputes between parties after a contract has been signed are not unheard of, but nor are they worryingly common. Huge delays in the courts and the high cost of litigation make arbitration and, increasingly, mediation more popular avenues for resolving disputes. Both parties must agree to arbitration and the decisions of the arbitration court have the same validity as litigation decisions in the law courts.

## CORPORATE VERSUS LOCAL CULTURE

Due to the lack of a coherent, national business culture, many multinational companies operating in Poland have attempted to impose a Western-style corporate culture in the workplace. Such experiments have met with varying degrees of success. A strong corporate culture is often accepted by young, eager employees wishing to make a career for themselves and move up in the organization. Older, more experienced, and better-educated employees tend to view such a regime as manipulative and may react rather cynically to attempts to instill a corporate culture within the organization.

### Finding the Right Level of Formality

For foreigners finding the right level of formality in social situations in Poland can be tricky, and when business is involved it is of added importance. Polish managers with international experience will be comfortable doing business in an informal manner and will generally follow your lead. If you are in a senior position, or older than your Polish counterpart, and prefer to work on a first-name basis then it is up to you to propose this. In the reverse situation it's better to hold off.

## INTERCULTURAL MANAGEMENT

Many of the foreign managers in Poland have been working in their professions for longer than Poland has had a free market economy. By contrast, Polish managers tend to be much younger, with relatively little international experience. It may seem natural then that the foreign managers see themselves as having superior knowledge and greater experience than their Polish colleagues. Without even realizing it, many Western managers may behave in a manner that can be seen as patronizing by their Polish counterparts.

Despite the relative youth of many high-level managers in Poland, these are people who, for the most part, have worked very hard to gain their positions. Polish managers tend to be very well educated, and have an insight into the specific nuances of the local market that foreigners, regardless of their experience, cannot match. Western managers who realize that they can learn from their Polish colleagues, and who communicate this clearly, have the most fruitful business relations.

## WESTERN ARROGANCE

Academic research has shown that Polish managers consider arrogance on the part of Western managers to be one of the biggest obstacles to effective cooperation. In fact, what the Polish managers consider to be arrogance may simply be a lack of understanding of each other's way of doing things.

## Communication

Communication is the key to avoiding such misunderstandings. Explaining why you would like a Polish colleague or subordinate to do something is critical. Those foreign managers who maintain a clear, regular channel of communication with their Polish colleagues have the fewest problems. In the case of a Western manager dealing with Polish subordinates, it is important to regularly check the progress of their work and to do so in a supportive manner. The lack of this kind of communication can lead to a situation where information is kept from you and your own colleagues and subordinates become uncooperative.

Bucking the trend. Dominika Kulczyk is the billionaire founder of the Values Consulting Group.

## WOMEN IN BUSINESS

In the Communist period women had no difficulty with upward mobility in certain professions, but faced a brick wall in others. Today's situation is different. At the bottom rung of the ladder women do not face discrimination by employers, nor are they held back from promotion to low-level management positions. Here, however, the picture changes. There are notable exceptions, but business is generally seen as a man's game and those women who make it to the boardroom often feel that they are not treated as equal partners, especially by elderly male directors and managers.

Statistically, women are paid less than men for the same work and are far less likely to be in the upper income brackets. A wife going to work is still viewed by many Poles, in rural Poland in particular, as doing this in order to supplement the family income while the husband remains the main breadwinner.

Legislation exists to protect women against sexual discrimination, but attitudes change slowly.

# CHAPTER NINE

# COMMUNICATING

## THE POLISH LANGUAGE

The Polish language is a challenge for foreigners. Getting around the clusters of consonants is a little like negotiating rush-hour traffic. Just try buying a train ticket to Szczecin and you'll get the point. Or how about telling a receptionist you'd like to speak with Krzysztof Brzęczyszczykiewicz? And it gets worse. Remember Latin lessons from school? Polish, like Latin, uses declensions, various noun forms that change according to the case. Polish grammar has seven cases and three genders and the result is a language that can be difficult even for native speakers. A simple example: the noun *dom,* meaning house, can be written *dom*, *domem*, or *domu*, depending on its use in the sentence. The same rule applies to proper nouns such as the names of towns, countries, and people.

One thing to keep you going through this linguistic labyrinth, however, is that your attempts to speak Polish, no matter how pathetic, will be appreciated.

Poles are very proud of their language, and your attempts to use it will be seen as a sign of respect. Perhaps this is because very few people will actually expect you to make an effort. The Polish-language skills of many foreign businessmen are limited to ordering a drink, despite having lived in the country for years.

### *Do You Speak English? German? Russian?*

Civil servants, railway employees, bus drivers, and others you may have to deal with are notoriously bad at foreign languages. There is a joke about two traffic policemen in Warsaw. An English businessman, completely lost and in need of help, sees them and pulls over:

"Do you speak English?" he asks.

"*Nie*," replies one of the officers.

"*Parlez vous francais?*"

"*Nie*," replies the other officer.

"*Gavareet pa Rusku?*"

"*Nie.*"

The Englishman, realizing he is not getting anywhere, rolls up his window and drives on. Later, the two policemen are speaking about the situation:

"Do you think we should learn a second language?" asks one.

"Why?" asks the other. "Look at that foreigner. He speaks three and it doesn't help him."

Having said this, you will also find that many locals will be happy to have an opportunity to practice their English. There is the example of the foreign driver who was involved in a small car accident; even though he was at fault, the other driver was thrilled to have the chance to speak English as they exchanged insurance details.

The truth is that in major cities you can get by with English. If you need help with directions, menus, and the like, look for someone under thirty and there's a good chance they'll be willing and able to assist you. Just remember to leave them with your best attempt at "*Dziękuję*," (pronounced jen-koo-yea), or "Thank you."

Apart from English, German is fairly common in the west of the country and the Lake District (Mazury), as well as other parts that were historically part of Germany. German expatriates living in Poland say that there isn't any anti-German sentiment to speak of and they feel welcome in their neighbor's country.

If grudges from the Second World War are largely forgotten, the Cold War is another matter. Russian is widely understood, but attitudes among Poles toward Russian speakers can vary greatly. Russian lessons were obligatory in Polish schools up to 1989, but have now been largely replaced by English, German, and French. Feelings toward Russians have been further exacerbated by the conflict in neighboring Ukraine.

## CONVERSATION

Conversation is a joy for Poles and in a friendly, informal setting there is no need to feel inhibited about any topic. Even matters of religion or politics are not taboo. If any warning is needed it is in regard to criticism of Poland as a nation. As we have seen, the Poles find humor in even the darkest situations and often make jokes about their history or the current situation. As a foreigner, however, you should avoid such comments about Poland. Jokes about your own country, on the other hand, will probably be enjoyed and help to remove the possibility of being viewed as an arrogant foreigner.

### Volume

Poles, as with Italians, like to be heard. Many foreigners visiting Poland for the first time wonder why people always seem to be arguing, but for Poles animated exchange is part of normal conversation. Don't feel offended therefore if a Polish friend or colleague disagrees with you in a very vocal and expressive manner. It actually means that you have been accepted as an active partner in the conversation. Nationally, politics and the economy are the topics you can expect Poles to be most vocal about, although, depending on their interests, it could be any matter on which they have a strong opinion.

### Body Language

It is not only in terms of volume that the Poles are outwardly expressive. There is an old (and un-PC) joke that the best way to make an Italian stop talking is to tie up his or her hands. While the same tactic may not mute a Pole, it would certainly cause a speech impediment. Unlike the Southern Europeans, however, the Poles do not use a lot of specific gestures in conversation. This is good news for foreigners as there is less chance of inadvertently causing offense or confusion by the misuse of a hand gesture.

Poles will often lean forward in their chair, or even stand up, in order to add weight to a specific point they are trying to make. It is also common, particularly in informal conversation between men, to touch the other's arm or give a pat on the back to make a point, gain attention, or show recognition or agreement.

## Misunderstandings

Two instances of misunderstandings caused by linguistic similarities are the meanings of the simple words "no" and "thank you."

The Polish word "no" is equivalent to the English conversation fillers "hmmm," "yeah," "well," or "really." It is used so habitually that even bilingual Poles may well use the expression when speaking English without even realizing it. Don't be surprised then if, for example, your comment that the restaurant you chose for lunch is very nice is met with a smiling "no" by your Polish guest.

"Thank you" ("*Dziękuję*") is another potential source of misunderstanding. Regarding a simple yes or no question, English speakers understand "thank you" to mean "yes," as in: "Would you like a cup of tea?" "Thank you." Poles, however, regardless of what language is being used, would take this answer to mean "no." It is always best therefore to say "Yes, please" or "No, thank you." When asking such a question always make sure to ask for clarification when a Pole responds with "thank you."

### Formal vs. Informal Forms of Address Revisited

As we have seen, finding the right level of formality can be difficult for foreigners dealing with Poles. Poles begin a new relationship, business or personal, with a very high level of formality, referring to each other as Sir or Madam (*pan/pani*). As there is no equivalent to this in modern English, simply use Mr. and Mrs. followed by the person's surname until they propose that you call them by their first name. If you are the elder person or hold a higher position (especially in business), it will be your responsibility to propose communicating on a first-name basis. Do this only when, and indeed if, you feel comfortable with it.

## SENSE OF HUMOR

We've also seen that Poles like to laugh at themselves while at the same time retaining their pride in being Polish. This has complex social roots and foreigners should not attempt to join in jokes about Poland, which can be taken as criticism.

Polish humor is largely situation based, and they enjoy jokes based on stories rather than wordplay—the

Polish language doesn't seem to lend itself to puns and double entendre. They don't like slapstick, which is seen as childish and lacking in irony, and find it strange that anyone would laugh at such simple things as someone falling over. Polish jokes can be strangely offbeat and tangential.

### What Can I Get You?

A man walks into a bar and orders, "A beer with no flavor."
The bartender asks, "Without which kind? No raspberry flavor or no ginger flavor?"
The man thinks for a minute and decides, "I'll take the one without raspberry flavor, thanks."

## SWEARING

Swearing is common in Poland, although you probably won't understand any of it. As in most countries, however, who swears is important. Swearing can be a sign of someone's low social class and level of education, although, having said that, in informal situations swearing is common among all classes of young Poles.

English swearwords and curses are widely known in Poland, as with most of the world, but naturally do not carry the same force as their equivalents in

Polish. Don't be surprised therefore to hear such words or phrases used casually and out of context.

## THE "YES" CULTURE

Many foreigners spending an extended amount of time in Poland notice an aspect of Polish culture that can prove problematic. It seems that Poles prefer to say "yes" even when it may not be the most appropriate answer. This is especially the case with questions such as, "Is everything going well with that project?" The truth may be that work on the project has barely started, but the answer "yes" reflects the optimism that everything will go well rather than the current situation. It is important to remember that for Poles this is not at all a dishonest or deceitful answer. For them, if someone was really interested in the progress of a project, they would ask specific questions about it. In fact, because this kind of response is part of their culture, Poles are completely unaware that it could be misunderstood. They have as difficult a time understanding your perception as you have theirs.

## THE MEDIA

Since the end of the Communist regime in 1989, Poland has enjoyed freedom of press. In recent years, however, this freedom has come under threat from state-owned broadcasters. Perhaps as a result, Poles are increasingly turning to the Internet, which, according to a recent study, is the most popular source of news in the country, followed by television news and print media.

## TV and Radio

Television remains popular, with Poles watching on average more than 4 hours per day, although this figure is falling. State-owned television (TVP) news coverage has been heavily influenced by the government under the PiS party rule. As a result, a political divide has opened up between the right-wing TVP and the private, liberal-leaning TVN, which has recently overtaken TVP to become the country's most popular source of television news.

Radio in Poland is a mix of private and public operators. Among the most popular are the private stations RMF FM and Radio Zet, as well as a number of state-owned Radio Poland (Polskie Radio) national and regional stations. The most controversial of the nation's broadcasters is the hardline conservative and Catholic Radio Maryja. The station is known for its extreme anti-abortion, anti-LGBTQ, anti-feminist, anti-immigrant, and anti-neoliberal stance.

## Print

Poles have always been avid newspaper readers and this continues to be the case, whether online or in print. Since the fall of Communism the full spectrum of political opinion has been available. The leading liberal daily newspaper is *Gazeta Wyborcza* ("*Election Gazette*"), edited by the historian and former dissident

Adam Michnik. And if you can't read Polish, there are three established English-language magazines available both online and in print to help you out. *The Warsaw Voice*, *Warsaw Insider*, and *Warsaw Business Journal* all offer up-to-date information for expatriate residents and tourists in the capital. In addition there are various free tourist information magazines available in English from hotels, airports, train stations, and tourist information centers.

## TELEPHONE

Polish telecommunication systems today are much the same as in other European countries, a great improvement on the dreadful state of the infrastructure twenty years ago. Pay-as-you-go SIM cards can be bought in almost any kiosk or in cellular phone shops and should work in phones from other countries, providing an affordable alternative to prohibitive roaming charges. Travelers from within the European Union don't need to worry about roaming as they can use their existing call and data plans while in Poland at no extra cost.

An estimated 78 percent of Poles own a smartphone, many now opting out of a landline. Free Wi-Fi is widely available in large public buildings such as shopping centers, train stations, and airports as well as in many shops, cafés, and restaurants.

## Area Codes

The international dialing code for Poland is 48. International dialing codes are, for the most part, the same throughout Europe. The area codes of some of the larger Polish cities below apply only to stationary phones connected by landlines, of which there are fewer every year. Cell phone numbers don't require a domestic area code.

### POLAND AREA CODES

(inside Poland, from a stationary phone, begin with 0)

| | |
|---|---|
| Gdańsk | 58 |
| Katowice | 32 |
| Kraków | 12 |
| Poznań | 61 |
| Warsaw | 22 |
| Wrocław | 71 |

## *Komorki*

The Poles have a love affair with cell phones, *telefony komorkowy*, known simply as *komorki*. In a relatively short period these have evolved from being status symbols to "must have" items, regardless of one's age or income. Businessmen, housewives, schoolchildren, and retired folk can all be seen strolling around, chatting on their cell phones.

There are a number of cellular phone networks in Poland and all operate on the GSM standard, meaning that phones from other countries with a roaming option should work problem free. 5G networks are widely available throughout the country, and the service is reliable.

## INTERNET AND E-MAIL

Ninety-two percent of Polish households have a broadband Internet connection. Connection speeds have increased significantly as well and the gap with Western European countries has closed. As we've seen, cafés and restaurants often offer a free Wi-Fi service. Just ask your server for the password, or "*haslo*." There is usually free Wi-Fi available at larger train stations, shopping centers, and on public transportation.

### Online Communication

Instant messaging and video calling have become the standard means of communication for many Poles, and are commonly used in work and school settings as well as for messaging between friends and family members. The most popular platforms used for work-related purposes are Skype, Zoom, and Microsoft Teams. For communicating between friends and family, Facebook messenger, Viber, Signal, Telegram, and WhatsApp are most common. Online gamers in Poland use Discord and TeamSpeak.

Red mailbox of the state postal service.

## MAIL

The Polish postal system (Poczta Polska) is quite efficient and inexpensive. Its near monopoly on delivery services has been brought to an end by aggressive competition by private providers. In recent years, courier services such as DHL, UPS, and InPost have expanded their operations in Poland, providing self-service parcel dispatch and collection points as well as access to their services in convenience stores.

Post offices are located in practically every neighborhood and town and are normally open from 8:00 a.m. to 7:00 p.m., and all large cities have a post office open twenty-four hours. In addition to sending mail, you can purchase money orders and exchange currency.

Most post offices now have an automated number system to eliminate the long lines. Simply take a number from the dispensing machine upon entering, then wait for your number to be displayed above one of the windows. To send a letter or package by air mail, ask for *lotnicza* or the international standard, *par avion*. You must also affix a blue *lotnicza* sticker, which you will find in baskets on all counters. Unfortunately, it is unlikely that you will find anyone working at the post office who can assist you in English.

## CONCLUSION

As we have seen, Poland retains much from its history, both ancient and recent. The changes that have swept through the large cities in the last fifty years have left much of the countryside, where life moves at a far slower pace, seemingly untouched. However, all of Poland's history—the glory and the oppression, stagnation and resurgence—has been absorbed into the country's cultural fabric.

Although modern Poland may lack cultural diversity, its cosmopolitan past has left its mark, with Germans, Jews, French, Italians, Russians, and Tatars all leaving traces in Polish art, architecture, cuisine, folklore, and myth.

Individual Poles, such as Copernicus, Marie Curie, Frédéric Chopin, Joseph Conrad, and Roman Polański, have contributed greatly to

Western science and culture. As a nation, Poland gave the world one of its first written constitutions and, more importantly, the knowledge that a people can endure any hardship and start again to rebuild their lives and their country.

This book offers you a cultural compass to help you discover for yourself something of the richness of the Polish experience and way of life. Your journey will be both exciting and rewarding. *Witamy w Polsce*!

# USEFUL APPS

**BlaBlaCar**
Poland's principal ride-sharing app. Register as a driver or passenger and share rides on your usual short and long distance routes.

**e-Toll**
Convenient payment app for Poland's motorway toll roads.

**Google Maps**
Reliable route planning throughout Poland that includes all modes of transportation.

**JakDojade**
A useful app for route planning within Poland, with schedules for all methods of public transportation. Additionally, tickets can be purchased using the app.

**Food and Shopping**

**Allegro**
This eBay equivalent is the most popular online shopping portal in Poland.

**Booksy**
Book beautician, hairstylist, and physical therapy appointments.

**Frisco**
One of many online-only supermarket shopping and delivery platforms.

**Glovo**
Delivery app for food, home goods, and other necessities.

**Pyszne**
Poland's most popular food delivery app.

**Communication and Socializing**

**Babbel Polish**
Learn Polish online. Free taster sessions available but operates a monthly subscription.

**Badoo, Tinder, and Sympatia**
Three of Poland's most popular dating apps.

**Viber, WhatsApp, and Facebook Messanger**
The most widely used messaging apps in Poland.

**DIC-o Polish-English**
Free offline dictionary.

# USEFUL WEBSITES

**www.biznes.gov.pl/en**
Polish Government information and services website for entrepreneurs, with information regarding working and running a business in Poland.

**www.cia.gov/cia/publications/factbook/geos/pl.html**
CIA World Factbook—Poland. An excellent source for concrete facts in a quick reference format.

**www.lot.com**
LOT—Polish National Airline. Check schedules and book international and domestic flights.

**www.orbis.pl**
Orbis—National hotel company and tour operator (available in English). Book hotels and tours.

**www.poland.gov.pl**
Official Polish Government website (in English). A user-friendly site offering an interesting introduction to the country and its people.

**www.pkp.pl**
PKP—Polish National Railway homepage (available in English). Check the Intercity and local train timetables.

**www.thenews.pl**
Polish state radio's English-language service with reliable news updates available as both text and podcasts.

**www.warsawvoice.pl**
The Warsaw Voice—English-language weekly newspaper. A good source for keeping up to date with current affairs and events in Poland.

**www.warsawinsider.pl**
Warsaw Insider—English-language monthly magazine. This has a great index of restaurants, pubs, cafés, theaters, etc. as well as ex-pat clubs and organizations.

**www.wbj.pl**
Warsaw Business Journal—English-language business weekly. Business and general news as well as good restaurant reviews.

# FURTHER READING

Aitken, Ben. *A Chip Shop in Poznan: My Unlikely Year in Poland*. London: Icon Books, 2020.

Czerniewicz-Umer, Teresa, Malgorzata Omilanowska, and Jerzy S. Majewski. *Poland* (Eyewitness Travel Guides). New York: DK Publishing Inc., 2019.

Davies, Norman. *God's Playground*. Volumes 1 and 2. New York: Columbia University Press, 2005.

Davies, Norman. *Heart of Europe: The Past in Poland's Present*. Oxford: Oxford University Press, 2001.

Davies, Norman. *Rising '44: The Battle for Warsaw*. New York: Viking Books, 2004.

Kapuscinski, Ryszard. *Nobody Leaves: Impressions of Poland* (Penguin Modern Classics). London: Penguin Classics, 2019.

Knab, Sophie Hodorowicz. *Polish Customs, Traditions, and Folklore*. New York: Hippocrene Books, 1996.

Lukowski, Jerzy, and Hubert Zawadski. *A Concise History of Poland* (2nd edition). Cambridge: Cambridge University Press, 2006.

Michener, James. *Poland*. New York: Fawcett Books, 2015.

Olson, Lynne, and Stanley Cloud. *A Question of Honor: The Kościuszko Squadron: Forgotten Heroes of World War II*. New York: Knopf, 2003.

Richmond, Simon et al. *Poland* (9th edition). Australia: Lonely Planet Publications, 2020.

Salter, Mark. *The Rough Guide to Poland* (8th edition). London: Rough Guides, 2018.

Szpilman, Wladyslaw. *The Pianist: The Extraordinary True Story of One Man's Survival in Warsaw, 1939–1944*. New York: Picador, 2002.

Terterov, Marat, and Johnathan Reuvid (eds). *Doing Business with Poland* (4th edition). (Global Market Briefings). London: Kogan Page, 2005.

Tokarczuk, Olga. *Drive Your Plow Over the Bones of the Dead*. (2nd edition). London: Fitzcarraldo Editions, 2018.

Zamoyski, Adam. *The Polish Way: A Thousand-Year History of the Poles and Their Culture*. New York: Hippocrene Books, 1993.

# PICTURE CREDITS

# INDEX